C/C++ Treasure Chest

A Developer's Resource Kit of C/C++ Tools and Source Code

Victor R. Volkman

R&D Books
Lawrence, KS 66046

b1110454

R&D Books
an imprint of Miller Freeman, Inc.
1601 West 23rd Street, Suite 200
Lawrence, KS 66046
USA

Distributed in the U.S. and Canada by:
Publishers Group West
P.O. Box 8843
Emeryville, CA 94662
ISBN: 0-87930-514-2

 **Miller Freeman**
A United News & Media company

Preface

This book represents the culmination of the work of hundreds of developers over the past 17 years. Each has made their own unique contribution of a C or C++ library, tool, or application. The mission of the C/C++ Users' Group (CUG) is to publicize and distribute user-supported software. *User-supported software* is a term coined by Robert Ward, the first steward of the C/C++ Users' Group. *User-supported* means that people using the software are not passive but actively collaborating to improve and update the software. This can happen only when the source code is made freely available. The CUG promotes user-supported software through low-cost distribution and publicizes it with help from the *C/C++ Users Journal*. This book ties up all of these efforts into a single, easy-to-use source of software, documentation, and indexes.

What is the CUG?

I have asked myself this question many times during the past five years of my tenure as Acquisitions Editor. First, let's look at what the CUG *was*:

The origins of the CUG are as humble as those of any computer user group. Initially, the CUG volumes were distributed on 5-1/2" and 8" floppy diskettes that held approximately 160Kb. More than 100 different diskette formats were then in use. At that time, the most common hardware systems were the Z-80 computers (8-bit) with 64Kb RAM and the fledgling CP/M operating system. The ANSI C standard was a decade away, and portability could be difficult. The CUG published a small quarterly known as *The C Users' Group Newsletter.* Today's *C/C++ Users Journal* (http://www.cuj.com) follows directly from the original newsletter.

Fast-forward nearly two decades: the CUG was one of the first adopters of the CD-ROM as an archival distribution mechanism. It is this universal storage medium that has allowed the source code to remain redistributable and usable for today's generation. Diskette distribution was recently phased out for CUG volumes due to the overwhelmingly better economies of CD-ROM. The layout of the CD-ROM is discussed in Appendix B.

The CUG has come to rely on the Internet for nearly all of its activities: finding new sources, publishing indexes, and personal contacts with members. The CUG Web site http://www.HAL9K.com/cug is a volunteer operation that provides electronic indexes to all volumes by Author, Subject, Language, Platform, and Volume #. The

CUG now searches the Internet regularly to bring the best and most portable code from around the world to you. If you've got something to share, we'd like to hear from you too. See Appendix A for the paperwork needed to submit your code today.

Victor R. Volkman
(e-mail `sysop@HAL9K.com`)
January 2, 1998

Table of Contents

Quick Overview of Volumes by CUG Catalog

Volumes 100–199: 1981–1986

101–148: CP/M, many are specific to Z-80/8080/6800 CPUs
149–199: CP/M and MS-DOS 2.0

Volumes 200–299: 1987–1989

MS-DOS predominates, less CP/M, some UNIX

Volumes 300–399: 1990–1993

MS-DOS, UNIX, OS/2, DEC VAX, some Atari and Amiga
First C++ volumes

Volumes 400–478: 1994–present

MS-DOS, UNIX, Windows, some OS/2
Many C++ volumes

CUG CD-ROM Volumes Listed by Topic

- String and Text Processing

- System Programming

- Text Windowing

- Tutorials

CUG Volumes 400–499

CUG 400   Sockets++: Socket Class Library

BSD UNIX sockets have been growing in popularity since their first appearance in 4.1cBSD UNIX release for DEC VAX-11 in 1982. Today, sockets can be found in nearly all BSD derivatives and even in MS Windows. BSD sockets emulate file descriptors as an extension of the UNIX file I/O system. Thus, you can call the standard library functions, such as read() and write(), to receive and transmit data. Since network communications requires more control than the file descriptor functions alone can provide, several new functions were added. For example, establishing a connection requires details about hosts, ports, protocols, and other options that simply cannot be expressed by open() alone. For a discussion of BSD sockets, see *Internetworking with TCP/IP*, Volume III; Englewood Cliffs, NJ; Prentice Hall; 1996; ISBN 013260969X.

Socket++, by Gnanasekaran Swaminathan (Centreville, VA), is an iostream-like class for UNIX and inet sockets, pipes, and socketpairs. Socket++ classes are more effective than directly calling the underlying low-level system functions. Since Socket++ has the same interface as the LibG++ iostream (e.g., cout and cin), it automatically performs type-safe input and output. Even though Socket++ is very easy to use, it supports a full complement of socket options, including error reporting, debug mode, keepalives, routing, broadcast datagrams, out-of-band data, and buffer resizing. Socket++ includes a mechanism for handling timeouts gracefully as well. Socket++ runs on many UNIX platforms, including Sun Sparc, IBM RS/6000, DECstation, and SGI Indigo boxes. Socket++ v1.11, released on 06/13/95, is available as CUG #400.

Specifically, the following classes are provided:

sockbuf Class::	Socket streambuf class.
sockAddr Class::	Base class for socket addresses.
sockinetbuf Class::	Socket class for INET address family.
sockinetaddr Class::	Address class for INET address family of sockets.
sockunixbuf Class::	Socket class for UNIX address family.
sockunixaddr Class::	Address class for UNIX address family of sockets.
sockstream Classes::	I/O socket stream classes.
pipestream Classes::	I/O stream classes that provides pipe, socketpair, and popen facilities.

Support Resources

FTP: ftp://ftp.virginia.edu/pub/

CUG 401   SGPC: Simple Genetic Programming in C

SGPC, or Simple Genetic Programming in C, by Walter Alden Tackett and Aviram Carmi, supports the Adaptive Automatic Program Induction method defined by Koza and Rice (Stanford University). The Koza and Rice method generates LISP programs designed to solve problems specified by the user. Tackett and Carmi have produced SGPC by porting the underlying algorithm for program creation from LISP to C. Thus, SGPC is a C program that generates LISP genetic programs as its output. Since SGPC is now available in C, it offers greater portability and a speed improvement of 25 to 50 times that of LISP programs, according to Tackett and Carmi. One notable improvement over the original is the ability to handle multiple populations. SGPC has been successfully built on many UNIX workstations, including Sun Sparcs, DECstations, HP-UX, and SGI Indigo. SGPC version 1.0 is available as volume #401 in the CUG Library.

For a complete description of genetic methods, see *Genetic_Programming* by John R. Koza (MIT Press, 1992). For other reading, see a paper delivered by Tackett entitled "Genetic Programming for Feature Discovery and Image Discrimination" for *Genetic_Algorithms: Proceedings of the Fifth International Conference (GA93)*, S. Forrest, Ed., Morgan-Kaufman 1993.

Problem definition takes place within three predefined files, named `setup.c`, `fitness.c`, and `prob.h`. Since each problem uses the same filenames, you'll need to have a separate subdirectory for each problem. SGPC includes an example set to solve Koza's simple regression problem and the ADF problem with a simple two-class dendritic classifier.

Specifically, `setup.c` contains function table and the functions it references as well as the terminals table. Next, `prob.h` must contain prototypes for the user-defined functions. Last, `fitness.c` contains functions to evaluate and validate populations and trees, early termination, and definition of the fitness (training and test) cases.

Support Resources

e-mail: gpc@ipld01.hac.com
FTP: ftp://ftp.aic.nrl.navy.mil/pub/galist/src/ga/

CUG 402   CForms: Builds Interactive Forms

CForms, by Lars Berntzon (Stockholm, Sweden), is a tool for building interactive forms–driven applications. CForms applications can run on any type of library supported by the "curses" library. CForms uses a language-based design to define forms. An application may contain C source modules, field pictures, field definitions, literals, and events. CForms applications must be compiled with the CFC compiler and linked with the CFL linker. CForms runs on most UNIX SYSV compatible platforms including SunOS, Dell-SVR4, and Diab SYSV.3. It requires a curses library and yacc or GNU Bison. CForms v2.1 is available as volume #402 in the CUG Library.

A CForm application consists of modules containing "pictures" to handle the various functions in the application. A picture in turn consists of fields and text literals describing the appearance. Fields are named regions of the screen used for input and output. Fields have attributes for type, size, and event-handling functions. Before creating a picture, you must first create a viewport. A viewport describes the width, height, and position on the real screen where the picture will appear.

You may specify field positions in absolute or relative coordinates. Alternately, you may ask to Center on a particular row or column or use Max to place it on the furthest row or column. CForms fields can be numeric, character, or alphanumeric. Last, a field can have any combination of the following modifiers: protected (read-only), forbidden, uppercase, highlighted, and invisible.

CForms shows its flexibility and ease of operation best in its event handling. Each field can have special handling for any of the following events: Key, Refresh, Draw, Left, Entry, and Exit. CForms includes a library of more than 30 functions for handling the most common types of event processing. For example, the function `fld_ismodified()` will tell you if the user actually changed anything.

The Key event allows you to intercept each keypress as the user types along in the field. CForms supports an extremely extensive set of keys including function keys, editing keys, numeric keypad function keys (e.g., SUN), and special-purpose keys (e.g., HELP key). Many keys have separate shift-state identifications (e.g., Shift-Delete-Char). However, Control keys and Alt keys are not supported.

CUG 403   Small Matrix Toolbox for C

Patrick Ko Shu Pui (Tai Po, Hong Kong) contributes the SmallMatrix Toolbox for C programmers. The toolbox is a set of C functions for matrix creation, arithmetic, inversion, and solving linear equations. This product has been released as shareware. Although you may freely use it for academic purposes, commercial users must register with the author for $25. The Small Matrix Toolbox for C v0.41 (released 09/23/93) is available as CUG volume #403.

The toolbox includes an abstract data type called MATRIX plus 18 functions for manipulating MATRIX objects. Specifically, the toolbox supplies these functions, where "M" denotes a MATRIX object:

Toolbox Function	Purpose
M = mat_fill(M, type)	Fill a matrix.
MatCol(M)	Tell how many columns.
MatRow(M)	Tell how many rows.
M = mat_colcopy1(M1, M2, j1, j2)	Copy columns between matrices.
M = mat_copy(M)	Duplicate a matrix.
fgetmat(M, fileptr)	Read matrix from an open file.
M = mat_dump(M)	Write matrix to stdout or file.
M = mat_add(M1, M2)	M = M1 + M2.
M = mat_mul(M1, M2)	M = M1 * M2.
M = mat_inv(M)	Compute inverse matrix.
M = mat_tran(M)	Find the transpose of matrix.
M = mat_submat(M, i, j)	Create a submatrix by deleting row,col.
mat_cofact(M, i, j)	Return cofactor of matrix[i,j].
mat_minor(M, i, j)	Return minor of matrix[i,j].
mat_det(M)	Return determinant of matrix.
M = mat_lsolve(M1, M2)	Solve linear equation M1 * X = M2.
M = mat_lsolve_durbin(M1, M2)	Levinson-Durbin method.
M = mat_SymToeplz(M1)	Create symmetric Toeplitz matrix.

The algorithms themselves are well documented and referenced. Ko draws from established computer science texts by Boas, Atkinson, Saito/Nakata, and Aho/Hopcroft/Ullman.

The Small Matrix Toolbox can be compiled on most UNIX workstations as well as Borland C++ on MS-DOS. The toolbox provides makefiles for both UNIX and MS-DOS environments.

CUG 404   Bison++: YACC for C++

Alain Coetmeur of the Informatique-CDC (Arcueil, France) presents two new packages that bring traditional UNIX tools into the 90s: Bison++ and Flex++. Coetmeur's Bison++ is derived directly from GNU Bison, the popular replacement for the UNIX utility called YACC (Yet Another Compiler Compiler.) Since its introduction two decades ago, the YACC software interface remains the most popular for developing compilers, assemblers, and other text-processing applications. Any language that can be handled by a LALR(1) parser is a good candidate for YACC use.

Bison++ injects C++ classes into the established YACC software interface while retaining downward compatability with programs that use the older C interface. This both makes the YACC software interface much more attractive for new C++ applications and gives a definite migration path for older C applications. Bison++ v1.21-7 (released 11/18/93) is available as CUG #406. The version number decodes to Revision 7 of Bison++ as integrated with GNU Bison 1.21.

Bison++ compiles on most UNIX workstations and includes the ubiquitous GNU "configure" utility to generate appropriate makefiles for your workstation. Additionally, Bison++ claims compatability with Microsoft C++ (makefile included) and Borland Turbo C++ (makefile not included).

Since Bison++ is a superset of Bison, the archive includes complete Bison documentation as well. The documentation for Bison++ is provided in both GNU texinfo format and postscript.

Support Resources

FTP: `ftp://ftp.th-darmstadt.de/pub/programming/languages/C++/tools/flex++bison++/`

CUG 405   Flex++: Lexical Analyzer for C++

Coetmeur's other contribution to the CUG Library is the Flex++ package. Like Bison++, Flex++ retains downward compatability with existing C programs while offering the benefits of C++ classes. Coetmeur's Flex++ is derived directly from GNU Flex ("Fast Lex"), the popular replacement for the UNIX utility called Lex. Since its introduction two decades ago, the Lex software interface remains very popular for developing front-end lexical analyzers for YACC and standalone text-processing applications. A Lex solution is ideal for matching both simple and complex patterns of characters.

Flex++ injects C++ classes into the established Lex software interface while retaining downward compatability with programs that use the older C interface. This both makes the Lex software interface much more attractive for new C++ applications and gives a definite migration path for older C applications. Flex++ v2.3.8-6 (released 11/18/93) is available as CUG #407. The version number decodes to Revision 6 of Flex++ as integrated with GNU Flex 2.3.8.

Flex++ compiles on most UNIX workstations and includes the ubiquitous GNU configure utility to generate appropriate `makefiles` for your workstation. Additionally, Flex++ claims compatability with Microsoft C++ (`makefile` included) and Borland Turbo C++ (`makefile` not included).

Since Flex++ is a superset of Flex, the archive includes complete Flex documentation as well. The documentation for Flex++ is provided in both GNU texinfo format and postscript.

Support Resources

FTP: `ftp://ftp.th-darmstadt.de/pub/programming/`
        `languages/C++/tools/flex++bison++/`

CUG 406   ATOC and DISKED

CUG 406A   ATOC: ANSI-to-K&R Backwards Translator

Mike Rejsa (Brooklyn Park, MN) submits his translator for converting ANSI-style C code and declarations to older Kernighan and Ritchie (K&R) syntax. Most C programmers have switched over to ANSI-style coding techniques within the last two or three years. The ANSI syntax allows for more comfortably readable code and brings you closer to what you really wanted to write. For example, declaring parameters in the prototype and use of `const`, `signed`, and `volatile` storage class modifiers. However, in the course of maintaining older UNIX systems, sooner or later you may have to handle the inelegant business of removing ANSI C specific constructs accurately from a newer source. ATOC v1.08 (released 11/15/93) has been designated CUG #406A.

ATOC translates ANSI programs back to a K&R compiling source stream. The CUG volume includes an MS-DOS executable (14Kb), but the ATOC source should compile easily on other platforms. ATOC itself is written in K&R C, so that you may retarget ANSI C programs from older or newer platforms. Here's a short summary of command-line options:

```
Usage: ATOC [-e] [-i] [-il] [-t] [-v] infile [ outfile ]
```

Examples of usage:

```
ATOC file.c            (convert and output to display)
ATOC file.c out.c      (convert and save)
ATOC -v file.c out.c   (convert and save with - V option)
```

The -e option will cause enumerations to be left alone. Some K&R compilers support enumerations.

The -i option will cause #include files to be included, converted, and placed in the output stream. Use ATOC without -i for simple one-time conversion, as when you have an ANSI program that you want to permanently convert to K&R style. Use ATOC with -i when you are maintaining ANSI code and wish to convert an included header "on the fly" each time you recompile using your K&R compiler.

The -il option is just like -i except that only the #include files (those whose name is in " " characters) are included and converted inline. If an #include filename is in <> characters, it is left as a normal #include statement. (These are often header files that come with the compiler, and as such would not be ANSI-C.)

The -t option will cause trigraphs to be left alone. (Note: If an older compiler supported trigraphs, they may not be ANSI-standard trigraphs and would therefore pass through ATOC unchanged anyway.)

The -v option will cause voids to be left alone. Some K&R compilers support the void data type. (Note: A void used to indicate an empty function parameter list (e.g., int func(void)) is always removed, even when using the -v option.)

CUG 406B DISKED: Sector-Level DISK EDitor for MS-DOS

Greg Jennings (Falmouth, MA) presents his MS-DOS DISK EDitor for low-level debugging and maintenance of floppy disks and hard disks. DISKED is a simple-to-use disk editor and data recovery program for PC-compatible computers. It allows the editing of any sector and the saving of sectors to a file. DISKED provides a way to recover data from disks with a damaged BOOT sector, damaged FATs, and damaged directory areas, allowing the saving of otherwise lost data. Jennings intends DISKED to be very easy to learn and to use. Commands have been abbreviated to as little as one letter for simplicity. DISKED v2.5 (released 01/14/94) has been designated CUG #406B.

Although DISKED can recover an erased file's data, DISKED cannot unerase a file. DISKED also does not format or change any parameters of the format of a disk, fix bad sectors, or move files around. What DISKED does is to read, write, and store any available sector of a disk in a simple and easy, yet powerful and versatile way.

DISKED starts at the root directory sector in a combined command and edit mode. You can navigate with arrow keys as if you were simply paging through a word-processing document. As you move, DISKED displays each sector encountered.

It maintains two available areas for data: a sector buffer that holds selected sector's data and a file buffer that allows saving sector data for writing to a disk file. The sector buffer can be edited bytewise with debugger type commands and then written back to the disk. DISKED provides a spare sector buffer to which a sector can be stored and retrieved for copying to another sector.

You may save data by appending single or multiple sectors into the file buffer. The file buffer can then be observed and changed, written to a disk file, emptied, or more sectors appended or unappended. Any number of absolute sectors can also be written to a file.

DISKED is written 100 percent in C and can be built in any Microsoft or Borland C compiler environment. Please note that DISKED is protected by the GNU Public License with additional amendments by Jennings.

CUG 407   PSUtils: PostScript Utilities

PSUtils, by Angus Duggan (Edinburgh, Scotland), is an assortment of utilities for manipulating PostScript documents. Page selection and rearrangement are supported, including arrangement into signatures for booklet printing, and page merging for n-up printing. The complete collection of PSUtils Release 1-PL11 (June 1993) is available as CUG Library volume #407.

PSUtils have been compiled and tested on Sun-3 and Sun-4 machines in every version of SunOS from 4.0.1 to 5.1 (Solaris 2.1). Other UNIX configurations supported include HP 9000/375 machines under HPUX 7.0 and HPUX 8.0, Sequent Symmetry machines under Dynix 3.1.4 and PTX 3.2.0, and Decstation 3100 machines under Ultrix 4.0.

PSUtils is not a monolithic system, rather it is a collection of C programs, C shell scripts, and PERL scripts. Each utility has its own command-line interface and corresponding manual page. Briefly, the utilities are as follows:

Utility	Summary
psbook	Rearranges pages into signatures.
psselect	Selects pages and page ranges.
pstops	Performs general page rearrangement and selection.

Utility	Summary
psnup	Put s multiple pages per physical sheet of paper.
epsffit	Fits an EPSF file to a given bounding box.
getafm	Outputs PostScript to retrieve AFM file from printer.
showchar	Outputs PostScript to draw a character with metric info.
fixfmps	Filter to fix FrameMaker documents so that psselect etc. work.
fixmacps	Filter to fix Macintosh documents with saner version of md.
fixpsditps	Filter to fix Transcript psdit documents to work with PSUtils.
fixpspps	Filter to fix PSPrint PostScript so that psselect etc. work.
fixtpps	Filter to fix Troff Tpscript documents.
fixwfwps	Filter to fix Word for Windows documents for PSUtils.
fixwpps	Filter to fix WordPerfect documents for PSUtils.
fixwwps	Filter to fix Windows Write documents for PSUtils.

The PSUtils licensing scheme allows you to incorporate any part of the collection into your own products. Your only obligations are to attribute them to the original author and provide information on how their original sources may be obtained.

CUG 408   SNews: Threaded Usenet Newsreader for PCs

Daniel Fandrich (Clearbrook, B.C., Canada) offers his SNews threaded Usenet newsreader add-on for PCs running UUPC/extended. UUPC/extended is a shareware package that provides dial-up e-mail access to public networks such as the UUCP network and/or the Internet. SNews can be built using Borland Turbo C for either MS-DOS or OS/2. The CUG Library volume includes MS-DOS executable and full source. SNews v1.91 (released 08/25/93) is available as CUG volume #408. Simple NEWS is an news add-on for UUPC/Extended v1.11n or later. It is designed to handle Usenet news as a leaf node, offering a number of features, as described in the list following.

- Threaded news reading, which allows you to be much more selective about what you read, enabling you to cover many more newsgroups.
- When a cross-posted article is read, the news-reader marks all the other instances of the article as read, too.
- Separate rc files are kept for each user, which record the individual articles that you have seen. This is in contrast to some readers that simply record the highest article number read.
- Usual range of response facilities: follow-up news, reply by mail, forward by mail, and save article/thread to disk.
- The extract function (key "w") saves articles to a user-specified file in the UUPC mailbox format (with a header of 20 hex 01s). Thus, extracted news articles can be read with the mail program later, at the user's convenience.
- Built-in support for ISO 8859/1/2/3/4/9 character sets (RFC 1341 and RFC 1342) and a single-key interface to the metamail MIME decoder (or other user-specified program).
- Article storage in two files per newsgroup, rather than one file per article. This results in an enormous saving (up to 3:1) in disk space on disks with a default cluster size of 4Kb per cluster.
- Processing of batched compressed or uncompressed news. Control messages are not processed.
- Duplicate cross-posted articles are killed during the unbatch stage.
- Post articles are unbatched and uncompressed. You can post only to your "mailserv" — you cannot feed another site. Posting can be done only from within the news reader SNews.
- "Received date" oriented expire to maintain the news database.

CUG 409   SuperVGA VESA VBE Test Kit and Universal VESA VBE

Kendall Bennett of SciTech Software (Melbourne, Australia) submits his SuperVGA VESA VBE test kit and Universal VESA VBE. The SuperVGA VBE VESA test kit thoroughly tests and demonstrates the VBE BIOS calls. The Universal VESA VBE is a drop-in replacement for an existing VBE driver you might or might not already have. As you may recall, the Video Electronics Standards Association (VESA) has established criteria allowing interoperability of SuperVGA hardware and software. The VESA BIOS Extensions (VBE) provide the ability to address video modes beyond regular VGA (640x480x16) in a hardware-independent fashion. Although the test kit includes full source code, the shareware VBE replacement driver offers source code for an additional licensing fee from SciTech Software. Both are available as CUG volume #409.

The SuperVGA Test Library is a set of routines for working with SuperVGA video cards that have a VESA VBE compliant Video BIOS. This library was an offshoot from the development of the Universal VESA VBE, which is an installable TSR to provide VESA VBE video BIOS extensions for most SuperVGA cards. It is intended to show how to program the SuperVGA cards through the VESA VBE and uses some of the more powerful features that the latest standard include in your own software. It was not designed with speed in mind, but as an explanatory and exploratory tool.

The SuperVGA Test Library supports many of the extended features of today's SuperVGA adapters, such as the ability to set the read and write banks separately and support for extended page flipping. This is all done via the standard VESA VBE programming interface.

The SuperVGA test programs all call upon a single C library to access the SuperVGA using the VESA VBE programming interface. You can use this same library to provide SuperVGA support in your own applications, or you can take the source code for the library as a starting point and expanding on it.

You may already have a VESA VBE TSR for your video card, or your video card may have a VESA VBE compatible BIOS already, so why would you want to use this replacement TSR? Most TSRs, especially those for older SuperVGAs, implement only v1.0 or 1.1 of the VESA VBE programming interface (if any at all). Thus programs expecting to use advanced features of the new VESA VBE v1.2 standard will not work with the earlier TSR or BIOS.

What advanced features does this TSR provide that others do not? The Universal VESA VBE implements the VESA VBE 1.2 programming interface, which supports the following features:

- SuperVGA page flipping. High performance animation programs can use your card to full potential using the VESA BIOS to implement extended page flipping (for example, 1024x768x16 double buffered animation, or even 800x600x256 and 640x400x32Kb/ 64Kb on a 1Mb video card).
- SuperVGA virtual screens. Programs may set up a virtual display resolution of say 1024x1024 pixels, and smoothly scroll a window with less physical resolution around within this buffer.
- Support for the 32Kb, 64Kb, and 16 million color video modes. Also supports the industry standard 16 and 256 color video modes.

- Speed. The bank-switching code in this package tends to run faster than the routines embedded in the VIDEO BIOS of some video cards.
- Programs that know about the Universal VESA VBE protected-mode extensions can use the high-performance protected-mode programming interface provided by this TSR.
- Extremely small size. When the TSR is resident in your computer it requires only about 3Kb of memory, which is smaller than the size of most commerical VESA VBE TSRs. It may be loaded high to save even more memory.

The SuperVGA VBE test kit has few restrictions on the use of the source code. The Universal VESA VBE is shareware and requires a $15 registration after a 21-day evaluation period. Source code for the Universal VESA VBE can purchased separately for $50.

For more information about VESA VBE, see some of my tutorials in these other R&D Publications journals (available through Miller Freeman, Inc.):

Volkman, Victor R. "The VESA BIOS Extensions for SuperVGAs," *Tech Specialist*, December 1990, p. 12 (covers VBE v1.1).

Volkman, Victor R. "VESA's VGA BIOS Extension (VBE) Standard," *Windows/DOS Developer's Journal*, October 1992, p. 13 (covers VBE v1.2).

Support Resources

e-mail: KendallB@scitechsoft.com
FTP: ftp://ftp.scitechsoft.com

CUG 410   PART and WList

CUG 410A   PART: Partition Table and Hard Disk Analysis Program

Gary A. Allen, Jr., (Prentice Center, Queensland, Australia) submits his PART utility for examining the partition table and hard disk parameters under MS-DOS. PART works with all MS-DOS compatible hard disks and provides additional low-level information on Integrated Drive Electronics (IDE) disk controllers. Allen notes that although there are powerful partition editors available, all of them run the risk of accidently changing these critical disk parameters. Since PART is a read-only display, the partition tables remain secure at all times. PART includes full source in C and claims compatability with the Borland C/C++ compiler. PART v1.5, as released on 10/27/93, is available as CUG volume #410A.

Although PART is intended for use only with MS-DOS, you can still run the BIOS reporting functions under OS/2. However, you may not use the IDE controller interrogation functions in an OS/2 window. A typical PART display is shown in the following figure. If you have an IDE controller, you can also obtain several other vital statistics including model number, serial number, controller revision, 32-bit transfer compatability flag, controller type, controller buffer size, number of Error Correction Code (ECC) bytes transferred, and number of sectors processed on each interrupt.

--- Partition Table and Hard Disk Examination Program ---
Program written by Gary A. Allen, Jr.
Version: Mk 1.5 27 October 1993
(c) Copyright 1993 by Gary A. Allen, Jr.

BIOS reports 820 cylinders, 6 heads (tracks) and 31 sectors/cylinder for a total (unformatted) capacity of 78090240 bytes.

Part Type	Type Code	Boot Part	Beginning Side Cylinder Sector			Ending Side Cylinder Sector			Starting Sector	Number of Sectors
DOSbig	0x6	YES	1	0	1	5	818	31	31	152303
Empty	0	NO	0	0	0	0	0	0	0	0
Empty	0	NO	0	0	0	0	0	0	0	0
Empty	0	NO	0	0	0	0	0	0	0	0

PART has ended normally. If you are interested in more information about this program then type: part -h

CUG 410B   WList: Doubly Linked List C++ Class

William E. Hatch of Coleman Research Corporation (Greenbelt, MD) submits his C++ class library implementation of doubly linked lists. The wlist class is a doubly linked list that stores a generic pointer, void *, at each node. Pointers to functions that print and compare the objects pointed to at a node may be set within a wlist class instance. Subsequent use of the print or compare functions assumes that all of the nodes, within a wlist instance, point to the same type of object. The wlist class includes a self-testing program to verify functionality on your platform. The wlist class as released on 02/15/94 is available on CUG #410B.

The pulic interface for the wlist class includes several useful operations:

Function	Description
wlist::wlist()	Constructor.
wlist::~wlist()	Cestructor.
wlist::Size()	Return the number of list nodes.
wlist::DeleteAll()	Delete all list nodes, set size to zero.
wlist::Name()	Access and assign list name.
wlist::FirstData()	Access and assign data in first node.
wlist::LastData()	Access and assign data in last node.
wlist::CurrentData()	Access and assign data in current node.
wlist::NextData()	Access and assign data in next node.
wlist::PreviousData()	Access and assign data in previous node.
wlist::AppendData()	Creates new node with data and appends.
wlist::PrependData()	Creates new node with data and makes new head.
wlist::PreInsert()	Insert node with data before current node.
wlist::PostInsert()	Insert node with data after current node.
wlist::DeleteCurrent()	Deletes current node.
wlist::ExchangePrevious()	Swap data between current node and previous.
wlist::ExchangeNext()	Swap data between current node and next node.
wlist::Maximum()	Return node containing maximum data value.
wlist::Minimum()	Return node containing minimum data value.
wlist::Sort()	Create new list containing data sorted.
wlist::Reverse()	Reorder list from back to front.
wlist::Copy()	Duplicate copy of this list (level 1 copy).
wlist::SetPrintData()	Stores pointer for later printing.
wlist::SetCompareData()	Stores pointer for later sorting.
wlist::print()	Debugging style dump of list.

CUG 411   Vi IMproved (VIM) Editor

Bram Moolenaar (Venlo, Netherlands) contributes his Vi IMproved editor (VIM), which supports MS-DOS, Amiga, and most forms of UNIX. VIM claims near 100% of the functionality of the classic "vi" UNIX editor. VIM also includes many embellishments on the original ideas and thus adds unique functionality of its own. The CUG Library edition includes full source in C as well as pre-built executables for MS-DOS. VIM v2.0, as released 12/14/93, is available as CUG #411.

VIM supplies extensive documentation in many forms including: a UNIX man page, UNIX man source file, quick reference card, platform-specific implementation notes, VIM and vi difference list, and an extensive, 70-page ASCII reference manual. For those not familiar with vi's distinctive user interface, tutorial files are provided to get you up and running fast.

VIM's improvements are perhaps the best reason to try this innovative text editor. Here's an abbreviated list of some of Moolenaar's enhancements:

- Multi-level undo and redo.
- Repeat a series of commands with arbitrary complexity.

- Flexible insert mode allows arrow keys while editing.
- Visual marking of lines or blocks of text.
- Command-line editing makes long commands easier.
- Filename completion mode saves typing long filenames.
- Horizontal scrolling wider than the screen.
- True word-processor-style text-formatting options.
- Integrates with make for a mini-IDE environment.
- Edit or view any binary file.
- Edit files containing 8-bit ASCII.
- Dynamically load and run Vim script command file.
- Edit files up to 2 billion lines long.
- Much, much more.

CUG 412 AISEARCH: Artificial Intelligence Search Class

Peter M. Bouthoorn (Groningen University, Netherlands) submits his C++ search class library with artificial intelligence capabilities. AISEARCH is a tool for developing problem-solving software. Basically, the library offers the programmer a set of search algorithms that solve all kinds of different problems. When developing problem-solving software, the programmer should concentrate on the representation of the problem to be solved and not on the implementation of the search algorithm used. This AISEARCH implementation of a set of search classes may be incorporated in other software through C++ derivation and inheritance. AISEARCH can be built in MS-DOS with Borland C++ or MS C++ and on UNIX using GNU C++. AISEARCH, as released on 02/10/94, is available as CUG #412.

Specifically, AISEARCH implements the following search algorithms:

- depth-first tree and graph search;
- breadth-first tree and graph search;
- uniform-cost tree and graph search;
- best-first search;
- bidirectional depth-first tree and graph search;
- bidirectional breadth-first tree and graph search;
- AND/OR depth tree search; and
- AND/OR breadth tree search.

With AISEARCH, using a search method in your own programs is just a matter of deriving a class from the desired search class and filling in the necessary parts. Turning the representation of the problem into actual source code is also made easier because the library demands that certain functions be used (these virtual functions are called by several routines in the search library), which helps standardizing this process.

Although this package is a tool for developing problem-solving software, it is not only for programmers who are familiar with the concept of problem representation and search techniques. The document accompanying this package briefly describes the theory of problem solving in AI and explains how to use the search class library. Since it includes richly commented source code and demo programs, it is useful to people who want to get acquainted with the subject.

Support Resources

WWW: `http://ganesh.mit.edu/sanjeev/drim/ais.html`

CUG 413 Sound Blaster Tools and Sound Blaster Freedom Project

The original Sound Blaster card by Creative Labs, Inc., has become the industry standard for PC digital audio. Today, a plethora of Sound Blaster (SB) compatible cards are available from many vendors. Although SB cards have proliferated widely, the knowledge required to program and control their operation has not. The I/O and DMA access protocol are critical for developers creating MS-DOS based applications with SB audio.

CUG 413A Sound Blaster Tools

David Welch (Las Cruces, NM) contributes his collection of Sound Blaster Tools in C (CUG #413A). He provides highly detailed information and C code in Borland Turbo C for a variety of audio mini applications. Sound Blaster Tools v4 (released 12/11/93) is available on CUG #413A.

These tools provide a programming specification for the Sound Blaster and Sound Blaster Pro (DSP DAC/ADC only). As a bonus, it also provides some information and C code on programming for the PC Speaker. Since the source is code intended to be a basic example, high-speed ADC/DAC is not demonstrated. All examples use DMA channel 1 and I/O base address 220h. Accordingly, source may need slight modification to work on your PC. The CUG Library volume includes precompiled versions of all executables. Specifically, Sound Blaster Tools builds the following MS-DOS mini applications:

- `rawin.exe` — record a raw SB digital audio file (not `.voc`);
- `rawout.exe` — playback a raw SB digital audio file (not `.voc`);

- `waveinfo.exe` — provides a debugging type dump of a Windows digital audio `.wav` file;
- `wave.exe` — play a Windows digital audio `.wav` file;
- `rwave.exe` — re-sample a Windows digital audio `.wav` file;
- `voice.exe` — provides a debugging type dump of an SB digital audio `.voc` file;
- `sbinfo.exe` — reads current status of SB card including DSP version, mixer settings, volume of all input settings, master volume, and more; and
- `speaker.exe` — allows you to play SB digital audio `.voc` files through PC speaker.

Additionally, it includes programming specifications for various Intel chips available to all PC compatables: 8259 Programmable Interrupt Controller, 8254 Programmable Interrupt Time, 8237 DMA Controller, and others.

CUG 413B   Sound Blaster Freedom Project

Jeffrey Bird, Dept. of Electrical and Computer Engineering at the James Cook University of North Queensland (Townsville, Australia), contributes his Sound Blaster Freedom Project (SBFP). As moderator of the SBFP, he has collected an impressive array of technical information. Bird writes:

The aim of the Sound Blaster Freedom Project is to provide a cheap source of programming information for the Sound Blaster and other sound cards. Previously, programming a sound card has required a not inconsiderable investment in a developer's kit for each sound card. These developer's kits have been known to be terse and not well written. Our aim is to provide enough information to the general programmer to allow them to add sound card support to their software at minimal cost.

SBFP includes source code in C and assembler for these DOS mini-applications:

- `dacdma.exe` — Output to SB DAC using DMA mode (up to 64Kb only);
- `recdma.exe` — Record from SB DAC using DMA mode (up to 64K only);
- `dacdir.exe` — Output to SB DAC in single sample mode;
- `driver.exe` — Uses CT-VOICE.DRV to access the Soundblaster DAC channel;

- getvol.exe — Displays master, VOC, line, FM, and CD volume levels; and
- fmtest.exe — Defines an FM instrument and plays chromatic scale.

Additionally, SBFP includes technical documents on programming the FM Music synthesizer chips, Intel 8237 DMA Controller, and Sound Blaster voice file format (.VOC).

SBFP v3.0 (released 01/25/94) is available on CUG #413B. This version includes significant enhancements by Christopher M. Box, some of which are:

- added support for Sound Blaster 2.0 high-speed mode (this allows recording at 15 kHz and playback at 44 kHz);
- added code to permit recording of samples, as well as playback;
- updated dma_code.asm for 16-bit DMA and added start/stop control functions; and
- fixed the bug that caused sbdac.c to play one byte too many.

CUG 414   THE: Highly Portable Text Editor

Mark Hessling (Holland Park, Queensland, Australia) offers his own full-screen text editor similar to IBM's VM/CMS XEDIT and Mansfield Software's KEDIT. The THE text editor uses both command-line commands and key bindings to operate. It has currently been ported to SUNOS 4.1.x, Xenix-386, MS-DOS (Borland C++ and MSC), Esix 4.0.3a, ATT SystemV 3.2, Linux, 386BSD, and OS/2 2.1 (MSC, C Set/2, Borland C++). The CUG volume of THE includes full source in C and a prebuilt executable for use with MS-DOS. THE v1.5, as released on 01/12/93, is available as CUG #414.

THE includes extensive documentation in the form of a 70-page ASCII Command Reference manual. In encylopaedic fashion, it describes each command along with its syntax, compatability with XEDIT and KEDIT, implementation status, and pointers to related commands.

THE makes use of the powerful IBM VM/CMS REXX command language in any environment where it is available. THE uses the OS/2 REXX interpreter to execute macro files. An extensive interface exists between THE and REXX, giving THE the complete power of REXX. REXX support is also avaliable on UNIX systems and with DJGPP using Regina 0.05, a free REXX interpreter available from ftp://ftp.flipper.pvv.unit.no in pub/rexx. Details on integrating THE and Regina are included in the makefile.

CUG 415   Run Time Type Information Library for C++

Arindam Banerji (Dept. of Computer Sci. & Eng, University of Notre Dame) contributes his Run Time Type Information Library for C++. Run Time Type Information (RTTI) is a C++ language extension proposed by the ANSI C++ committee. The extension has now been implemented as part of many C++ compilers. However, it may be some time before every C++ compiler has the extension. Fortunately, Banerji's implementation of RTTI as a C++ library means that you can start taking advantage of it right away. His system is loosely based on the RTTI system demonstrated by Stoustroup in "The C++ Programming Language." RTTI for *C++* works *only* with UNIX-based C++ implementations due to file-naming conventions that are *incompatible* with MS-DOS. RTTI for C++, as released on 11/03/93, is available as CUG #415.

All classes in this RTTI system inherit from the CLASS base class. This allows public virtual inheritance to work. CLASS has very little functionality associated with it, although it itself has the RTTI scaffoldings neccessary for all users of RTTI. The narrowing facility (i.e., going from a base class pointer to a derived class pointer) depends on the use of CLASS.

The Type_info class is the core of the RTTI implementation. It is initialized once, per class. The constructors accept a list of the base classes and the name of the class. The typeid class provides an interface to the RTTI system and users get at the RTTI through this class. This class acts as a pass-through for the Type_info class.

The base_iterator class is initialized with the list of base classes. It allows the clients of the Type_info class to iterate through the list of bases. RTTI also includes demonstration code for string and trace classes.

For every class that uses the RTTI must use some scaffolding in both the declaration and the definition of the class. The declaration must contain the following:

- For every RTTI class, a static Type_info class needs to be created, as in static const Type_info info_obj.
- For every RTTI class, two functions must be created to retrieve Type information (one a virtual function and the other a simple function), as in:

```
virtual typeid get_info() const ;
static typeid info() ;
```

- In order to allow a base class pointer to be converted into its appropriate derived class pointer, the narrowing facility is provided.

```
static Type_info *_narrow(CLASS *) ; and
```

- In order for the narrowing facility to work in the presence of virtual public inheritance, every RTTI class defines a virtual function that returns its `this` pointer.

```
virtual void *get_this_ptr(void) const
```

CUG 416   SaltSoft Tools for Math and Graphics

Nigel Salt (Crayford, Kent, U.K.) contributes a variety of stand alone tools and libraries with source code in C for MS-DOS. This is the first time source code for many of these tools has been released. Some of the programs are written specifically for Borland Turbo C; others are intended for use with Microsoft C (MSC). All programs are shareware with reasonable registration fees ($15 or less) or donation-ware (whatever you feel is appropriate). The CUG Library volume includes the following programs in both source and executable format:

- DUMPNS — dumps a binary file in octal, hex, or decimal formats (MSC).
- GREPFV — finds text matching a regular expression in plain files or PAK, ARC, ZIP, LZH, or ZOO archives (MSC).
- PCSLIDE — Builds a color VGA presentation with large-screen fonts and bullets.
- VIDSTATE — Decodes and displays INT 10h, function 1Bh video state information (MSC).
- SPIRO — Spirograph simulator uses a still ellipse and a moving circle with a virtual pen at some position on (or beyond) its radius. The moving circle can be inside or outside of the still circle. The following figure shows a sample run of SPIRO.
- MATRIX — Complete function library for matrix manipulation. Includes scalar and mat multiplication, add, copy, transpose, determinant, invert, and solve as simultaneous equation. Includes mini-library of 3D transforms to translate, scale, and rotate (MSC). Additionally, the CUG Library volume includes other SaltSoft applications in MS-DOS executable without source:

  - 8pdj500 — Print eight pages of text on a single HP DeskJet 500 page.
  - 16to256 — Convert 16-color images to 256 colors (use with IMED256).

Sample run of SPIRO

- IMED256 — Design 256-color sprites and animate them.
- PCGDEM — VGA text and graphic font editor.
- TURGRA — Turtle-graphics interpreter for VGA (similar to LOGO).

The entire SaltSoft volume (as released on 02/16/94) is available as volume #416 in the CUG Library.

CUG 417   LIBFTP: Easy Interface to Servers

Oleg Orel (Institute for High Energy Physics, Protvino, Russia) presents his LIBFTP TCP/IP library. LIBFTP provides an easy callable interface for UNIX programs to talk with FTP servers as defined in RFC 959. The FTP (File Transfer Protocol) is the protocol of choice for transferring files over the Internet. You can use this library to write your own FTP client with a graphical user-interface or, perhaps, to provide the basis of a file-mirroring utility. LIBFTP works with most popular UNIX systems but cannot work with MS-DOS. LIBFTP (as released on 10/28/93) is available as CUG #417.

A full suite of functions provides the ability to have multiple FTP channels open simultaneously. A stream level interface allows for reading and writing using many popular stream functions, such as fgetc( ). You can also ask for directories to be created on the FTP server as well as send and receive files.

LIBFTP includes a 10-page User's Guide describing each of the function calls available. The documentation is provided in both English and Russian versions. Each appears in both Tex and PostScript printable format.

LIBFTP provides two very small examples that can be used to check out the library. FCP.C demonstrates copying a file between two FTP servers in stream mode (without opening intermediate files). GET.C uses a simple command-line interface to fetch a single file and then hang up the FTP connection. All C source code is provided with this volume. You can use the GNU C compiler or any compatible ANSI C compiler.

Support Resources

e-mail: Oleg.Orel@cern.ch
WWW: http://www.cn.cern.ch/~orel

CUG 418   RasMol Molecular Graphics

Roger Sayle (Dept. Computer Science, University of Edinburgh, U.K.) contributes his molecular graphics visualization system for UNIX XWindows and MS Windows. Specifically, RasMol is intended for the visualization of proteins and nucleic acids. It reads Brookhaven Protein Databank (PDB) files and interactively renders them in a variety of formats on either an 8-bit (see the following figure) or 24- to 32-bit color display. Documentation includes include online help, hypertext documentation, and the previous (dated) version of the PostScript user reference manual. RasMol v2.3 (as released on 03/04/94) is iavailable as CUG #418.

RasMol is intended for teaching and generating publication-quality images. The program has both a menu system and a full-featured command-line interface. Different parts and representations of the molecule may be colored or displayed in a number of formats independently. Currently supported formats include wireframe, ball and stick, backbone, space-filling spheres, and solid or strands ribbon models. The space-filling spheres may even be shadowed. The molecule may be manipulated using the mouse, the scroll bars, the interactive command-line, or may be manipulated from a dials box (if one is attached). The resulting image may be saved at any point in PostScript, GIF, PPM, Sun rasterfile, or Microsoft BMP formats. On a SparcStation, it can shadow a 10,000-atom space-filling protein in less than 10 seconds.

The current version of the program has been tested on sun3, sun4, sun386i, SGI, DEC & E&S mips based machines, DEC Alpha (OSF/1 and OpenVMS), VAX VMS (under Dec Windows), IBM RS/6000, hp9000, Sequent, compiled under both gcc and (typically) the native compiler. The version for Microsoft Windows requires theVisual C++ Compiler.

Phage CRO Repressor on DNA. Andrew Coulson & Roger
Sayle with RasMol, University of Edinburgh, 1993

The source code is public domain and freely distributable provided
the original author is suitably acknowledged. Although no formal registration is required, the author suggests a donation of $40 U.S. currency
or 25 pounds British currency for those who "appreciate the large
amount of work that went into RasMol."

Support Resources

WWW: http://www.umass.edu/microbio/rasmol/

CUG 419　An ODMG-93 Collection for UNIX

Dale Anderson (San Diego, CA) submits his a first release of the collections specified by Object Database Management Group-93 (ODMG-93). This work is based on the publication *The Object Database Standard: ODMG-93* (ISBN 1-55860-302-6). Although Anderson has no personal affiliation with the ODMG, this work nevertheless represents an important contribution to the dissemination of this conceptual model. His release contains collection classes (see Chapter 5), man pages for each method, and a test suite for almost all methods. The code itself has been tested on an HP/UX 9.0 C++ compiler and GNU C++, also on this platform. Anderson's ODMG-93 implementation for UNIX (as released on 03/02/94) is available as CUG #419.

This implementation does not include a mechanism for persistent objects. Instead, he intends this to be the "front end" of the specification, so that software developed today can easily integrate with an object-oriented database (OODB) in the future. Since the ODMG-93 specification intends to be independent of OODB implementations, no back-end database will appear in this implementation. Additionally, this implementation does not include an SQL parser, though such a parser may eventually be released.

Anderson's short-term goal is to develop a working model of the ODMG-93 class library that is as near to 100 percent compliance as possible. This model then becomes a tool to compare and contrast with the written specification and to experiment with alternatives that can then be proposed to the ODMG-93 working group. Over the long term, he hopes to continue to track extensions of the ODMG model as they occur.

This software fits the description in the U.S. Copyright Act of a "United States Government Work." This means it cannot be copyrighted. This software is freely available to the public for use without a copyright notice, and there are no restrictions on its use, now or subsequently.

CUG 420　VGAMAZE and Coerce

CUG 420A　VGAMAZE in 3-D

James L. Dean (New Orleans, LA) contributes his VGAMAZE tools written for MS-DOS VGA graphics with the Borland C++ 3.0 compiler. VGAMAZE displays mazes with square (SQRMAZE.CPP, see the following figure)or hexagonal rooms (HEXMAZE.CPP) in three dimensions on your monitor. It includes a template for one-dimensional virtual arrays. The plotting class can plot any surface z=f(x,y). An example program for surfaces (SPIKE.CPP) demonstrates that it is good for more than just mazes. The CUG Library volume includes all C++ source code and executables for SQRMAZE, HEXMAZE, and SPIKE. VGAMAZE v4 (as released on 02/27/94) is available as CUG Library volume #420A.

A square maze generated by VGAMAZE

When you start a maze program, you will be prompted for an 8- (or fewer) character random number seed. Usually, a different random number seed will produce a different maze. After the maze is displayed, press "S" to see the solution. A VGA (or SVGA) graphics card, a VGA monitor, and about 2Mb of Expanded memory or disk space are needed (for virtual memory).

VGAMAZE supports only the Large memory model. VGA3D.CPP uses Borland's GRAPHICS.LIB, so main programs must be linked with the library. See the Borland documentation on the utilities BINOBJ and TLIB for information on including EGAVGA.BGI in GRAPHICS.LIB.

Be advised that VGAMAZE performs an extreme amount of floating-point arithmetic and probably should not be run without a math coprocessor. On my Cyrix 80486DLC 40MHz machine (without math coprocessor) I waited for 28 minutes for VGAMAZE to complete its work. On a Pentium P5 120MHz machine, the same maze required only 40 seconds.

For HEXMAZE, do not optimize invariant code motion if you optimize common subexpressions; a bug in Borland C++ 3.0 causes incorrect code to be generated.

CUG 420B   Coerce: Graphics File Converter for UNIX

Tatsurou Sekiguchi (Department of Information Science, University of Tokyo, Japan) submits his Coerce program, which can convert many graphic file formats popular on BBSes in Japan. Specifically, it converts from one of MAG, PI, PIC, MAKI, PPM, PBM, ML1, and beta formats to one of MAG, PI, PIC, PPM, and beta formats. Coerce can be compiled on any Sun workstation running SunOS 4.1.3 with GNU C++ 2.4.5 or later. Others have reported good success compiling Coerce on MIPS and RS/6000 machines. Sekiguchi also includes source for a simple X Windows bitmap viewer. Coerce (as released on 02/24/94) is available as CUG Library volume #420B.

"Beta format" is an internal representation of graphic images in Coerce, which is very similar to VRAM images of X68000 (SHARP) or FM-TOWNS (Fujitsu). The format is often used for debugging. PBM is the Portable BitMap format and supported by a wide range of systems. Coerce is aimed to accelerate traffic of graphic images between BBS and Internet.

Coerce is a synthesis of all converters, which can be used as an alternative of each converter. For instance, in order to convert .mag format to .pic format, type:

```
% coerce -mag +pic foo.mag
```
Options of coerce:

-{mag,pi,pic, maki,ppm,pbm,ml1,beta}	Specify the format of input images.
+{mag,pi,pic,ppm,beta}	Specify the format of output images.
-notadjust	Prevents adjusting an aspect ratio of pixels for PIC format images.
-stdin	Indicates an input image is read from standard input.
-stdout	Indicates the result is sent to standard output.

-o [name]	Specified the output file name.
-quiet	Prevents messages from being written.

Porting to other environments and other machines is welcomed. Any trial to incorporate new facility to save/load images in another format is also welcomed. There is already a patch for xv that enables it to load mag and pic format images. It is an interesting attempt to combine coerce with xv.

Coerce includes a part of source files of PiFM v0.16 which was written by Takashi Nawashiro. Separate permission was obtained to use and redistribute it. Sekiguchi waives the copyright on this software. He allows that you can use/modify/redistribute this package freely, even for commercial purposes.

Support Resources

e-mail: cocoa@is.s.u-tokyo.ac.jp

CUG 421   RFV VGA Graphics Animation Demo

Thomas Hagen (Trondheim, Norway) contributes his RFVDEMO collection of high-speed VGA animation demonstrations for MS-DOS. The animations require the Borland C++ 3.1 compiler. There are four main animation demonstrations included: bitmap-rotation routine, fractal zoomer, plasma, and voxelspace routine. These are in addition to lower-level support routines for keyboard handling, timer class, and others. RFVDEMO v0.1 (as released on 01/17/94) is available as CUG volume #421.

I was particularly impressed with speed of these demonstrations on my Cyrix 80486DLC 40MHz machine (without math coprocessor). The bitmap rotation appeared seamless, without flicker. The fractal zoomer showed the Mandelbrot set at a breathtaking speed, faster than some fractal videotaped productions I've seen. A utility called MAKEFRAC is also included, so you can design your own fractal animation sequences. The plasma literally oozes and flows across your screen (see the following figure). Last, the voxelspace uses shading and perspective to give you a realtime flyby over imaginary terrain.

RFVDEMO requires an 80386 or better CPU (486 recommended) and a register-level compatible VGA-card. The programs have fairly heavy MS-DOS low-memory requirements of 500 to 600Kb.

Hagen mentions that documentation has been kept to a bare minimum. He writes "The one thing you WON'T find, though, is verbose comments. You're pretty much on your own here!" Licensing is equally informal, since the source code has been released into the public domain. Hagen asks only for a postcard if you find the source code useful.

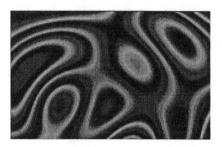

Output from dynamic "plasma" display

CUG 422   MICRO-C C Compiler

Dave Dunfield (Nepean, Ontario, Canada) submits an entire suite of tools from the MICRO-C C compiler development system. This includes the MICRO-C C compiler itself for MS-DOS, more than 85 useful sample programs with full C source, and a demonstration version of MICRO-C for embedded systems. MICRO-C is a tiny compiler that can run with less than 32Kb RAM and yet is highly independent of CPU and OS. Specifically, platform support is available separately for 68HC08, 6809, 68HC11, 68HC12, 68HC16, 8051/52, 8080/8085, 80x96, and 8096 CPUs, as well as the C-FLEA (a portable C virtual machine supporting any processor). The CUG Library volume includes a fully functional MICRO-C compiler executable built for the MS-DOS 80x86 environment. This version generates code in .asm format so Microsoft MASM, Borland TASM, or equivalent are required (not included). MICRO-C v3.14 (as released on 09/22/95) is available as CUG #422.

MICRO-C provides much more functionality than Small-C and its many derivatives. Specifically, MICRO-C supports all C statements, operators, and preprocessor directives as well as in-line assembler. MICRO-C includes data types for int, char, unsigned, struct, union, pointers, and typecasting. Saying it another way, MICRO-C gives you everything possible except for typedef, long, double, float, enumerated, and bit fields. The runtime library does include a long arithmetic package with arbitrary precision up to 256 bits.

Even if you're not especially interested in the MICRO-C compiler, you may wish to take advantage of the collection of more than 70 sample programs. Although there are simply too many to catalog here, I've listed two dozen of the most interesting.

Program	Description
CCREF	C source cross-referencing program.
COMEXT	Extract comments from C sources.
OBSCURE	Make C program unreadable (but it is still compiles).
PPC	Pretty Printer for C (source formatter).
CALC	A TSR programmers (HEX/DECIMAL) calculator.
CMOS	Read/Write/Verify CMOS RAM from/to/with disk file.
CSET	TSR map of IBM PC character set.
DIFF	Displays differences between text files.
GREP	Like UNIX grep search utility.
HEM	Hardware Exception Monitor TSR to trap unexpected ints.
LZC	Laser commander TSR to control HP-compatible printers.
MEMSAVE	Saves memory image to file.
MTERM	Tiny (10Kb) TSR ANSI terminal with XMODEM.
SHOWEXE	Displays information about a .exe file.
TFB	TSR File Browser.
VALIDATE	PD ver of McAfee's validate. Verify with two CRCs.
LAPTALK	A terminal program with script interpreter.
XMODEM	External file transfer program.
MICROCAD	Mouse-based drawing program.
FE	Font Editor.
ASM86	8086 assembler.
BASIC	A simple BASIC interpreter.
DIS85	8085 Cross Disassembler.
TTT3D	3 dimensional tic-tac-toe.

The PC compiler is completely free in the sense that no payment is required, and you may do whatever you like with your own programs compiled with it. That is, you still can't re-sell the tools, but you can use them in any way that you like. An optional $25 registration the latest copy, the source code to the libary, and a few other goodies. Highlights of v3.14 include:

- Changed compiler from `.com` to `.exe` (allows larger internal tables)
- Add #`if` and #`error` directives to MCP
- Fix to allow `sizeof()` in array declaration
- Fix to detect redeclarations differing in dimension
- Fix to prevent index being promoted with type of array

Support Resources

e-mail: `tech@dunfield.com`
WWW: `http://www.dunfield.com/downld.html`

CUG 423   RECIO, MIMEQP, ACCTPOST, RDCF, and BSPLINE

The CUG Library has always accommodated C/C++ archives both big and small. CUG volume #423 is an anthology of five outstanding but small source archives. William Pierpoint (Camarillo, CA) submits his comprehensive library for stream-style record I/O. Karl Hahn (Sarasota, FL) contributes a MIME binary encode/decode routines for use with email tools. Philip Erdelsky (San Diego, CA) releases both source for general ledger posting with 32-bit math library and a Reentrant DOS-compatible File System for embedded systems. Last, Keith Vertanen (Pine Springs, MN) sends his brief but succinct implementation of the BSPLINE rendering algorithm. Again, all five archives are available as CUG volume #423.

CUG 423A   RECIO: Record Input Made Easy

The RECIO library contains more than 50 functions and macros enabling file input where each line becomes a data record, and each record is subdivided into fields. Fields may be either character delimited or column delimited. The learning curve is simplified since many functions are based on analogous counterparts in `stdio`. RECIO is freeware and is protected by the GNU Public License. RECIO v2.00 (as released 04/16/94) appears along with several unrelated archives on CUG volume #423A.

Since virtually every program has to do input or output, the stdio library is very familiar to C programmers. Many functions in the recio library are analogous to the stdio library. This makes the learning curve easier.

Analogous stdio/recio components

stdio	recio
FILE	REC
FOPEN_MAX	ROPEN_MAX
stdin	recin
fopen	ropen
fclose	rclose
fgets	rgetrec
fscanf	rgeti, rgetd, rgets, ...
clearerr	rclearerr
feof	reof
ferror	rerror

RECIO includes a makefile only for Borland Turbo C, although other platforms should work too.

CUG 423B   **MIMEQP: A Better Encode/DDecode for E-mail**

MIMEQP (or MIME Quoted-Printable) encodes files that are mostly ASCII but contain some non-ASCII characters so that the encoded file is all ASCII. The characters that were ASCII remain so, so that the encoded file is human-readable. MIMEQP encoding also limits line lengths to 72 characters. It is useful for sending files that may contain non-ASCII through mail servers. MIMEQP is defined in RFC 1341. MIMEQP (as released on 05/22/93) appears along with several unrelated archives on CUG volume #423.

MIME is an acronym for Multipurpose Internet Mail Extensions. It builds on the older standard by standardizing additional fields for mail message headers that describe new types of content and organization for messages.

MIME allows mail messages to contain:

- multiple objects in a single message;
- text having unlimited line length or overall length;
- character sets other than ASCII;
- multi-font messages;
- binary or application specific files; and
- images, audio, video, and multi-media messages.

Encoding replaces all Control characters except \n and \t, all =s, and all characters that have an ASCII code greater than 127 with = XX where XX is the hex value of the ASCII. A substantial overview of the MIME standard by Mark Grand along with an MS-DOS executable is included with the CUG Library volume.

CUG 423C ACCTPOST: Simplifies General Ledger

The Plain Vanilla Posting Program II is a simple program that takes over three tedious accounting tasks: posting from the general journal to the general ledger, drawing a trial balance, and putting account balances into a report. The Plain Vanilla Posting Program II was written for the Compact memory model (near function, far data) in Turbo C 2.0 for MS-DOS. The author claims some source portability to UNIX variants as well. The Plain Vanilla Posting Program II (as released on 09/01/90) is included with unrelated source archives on CUG volume #423.

The only non-portable part of the program appears in arithmet.c, which contains embedded assembler code. This allows us to catch arithmetic overflows, which would be disastrous for an accounting application if undetected. Otherwise, it's just a simple 32-bit arithmetic package with only five operations: addition, negation, multiplication, and division by 10, and the computation of the remainder when a 32-bit number is divided by 10. The last two operations cannot produce overflows and might have been written in standard C. Porting to a machine with native 32-bit arithmetic should be simple.

Although the Plain Vanilla Posting Program II is copyrighted, there remains only one restriction. You may not sell the program or any program derived from it. You may give it away or charge a reasonable fee for media duplication, but may not charge anything for the software itself.

Support Resources

e-mail: pje@acm.org
WWW: http://www.alumni.caltech.edu/~pje/software.html

CUG 423D   **RDCF: Reentrant DOS-Compatible File System**

RDCF is a reentrant and ROMable DOS-compatible file system designed for use with floppy diskettes and hard disk partitions that do not exceed 32Mb in size. Also included is a simple disk caching package designed for use with RDCF. However, it may also be used separately. A DOS utility called FILES, written primarily to test RDCF, is included in both source and executable form. It performs a number of operations on DOS files, including some that cannot be performed from the DOS command line. For example, its `dir` command shows the remains of deleted files.

Complete C source code and documentation are included, including a fairly detailed description of the DOS file system.

RDCF is copyrighted, but it is freeware. You may copy it and pass it on freely, as long as you pass on the entire, unmodified package, with its copyright notices intact. You may not resell it, although you may charge a reasonable fee for diskette duplication, shipping, and handling.

Support Resources

e-mail: `pje@acm.org`
WWW: `http://www.alumni.caltech.edu/~pje/software.html`

CUG 423E   **BSPLINE: Classic Spline-Rendering Algorithm**

The spline is a mathematical construct from numerical analysis that is used to fit a curve to an arbitrary set of points. It has obvious uses in statistics and computer graphics rendering. For a description of spline theory and algorithm implementation, see *Elementary Numerical Analysis* by Kendall Atkinson (1985, John Wiley & Sons). The BSPLINE archive uses polynomial interpolation to return an array of coefficients to describe it. BSPLINE was written in C++ for the Borland compiler, though it uses few, if any, features of C++. The library uses function calls from the Borland Graphics Interface to render the BSPLINE on EGA or VGA displays. BSPLINE (as released on 03/11/94) is included with other unrelated archives on CUG volume #423E.

Support Resources

e-mail: `vertanen@cs.orst.edu`
WWW: `http://www.CS.ORST.EDU/~vertanen/`

CUG 424   ED Editor: Highly Portable Windowing Editor

Charles Sandmann (Houston, TX) submits the ED editor with a user interface based on the DEC VMS EDT editor. ED is a true multiplat-form editor and can be compiled and run on virtually any platform. It includes target-specific code for keyboard, screen, and TCP/IP han-dling. This allows it to run on UNIX (IBM RS/6000, Sun Sparc, HP, NeXT, or Alpha AXP machines), MS-DOS, Windows NT, and OS/2 environments with ease. ED can edit any kind of file in text, binary, or hexadecimal modes.

Some of the more interesting ED features include the following:

- multiple text windows;
- built-in file manager;
- editing by wildcards;
- calculator;
- automatic program indentation;
- parenthesis matching;
- box and columnar editing;
- insert and overstrike editing;
- sorting; and
- load/save files using FTP.

The ED documentation consists primarily of a 45-page ASCII help file. This help file can be invoked from within ED or searched using any standard text utilities you might have. The documentation assumes that you've had some exposure to the EDT editor that ED emulates or are willing to learn the basics.

The CUG Library volume of ED includes binaries built with the DJGPP edition of GNU C/C++ (MS-DOS with GO32 DOS extender). Also, full C source is provided. Distribution and use of the ED source code is covered by the GNU General Public License, Version 2. ED v1.5.7 (as released on 04/05/94) is available as CUG #424.

CUG 425   Portable Tar and LZPIPE

CUG 425A   Portable Tar: Read/Write Files, Floppies, QIC Tapes

Timor V. Shaporev (Moscow, Russia) contributes an extremely ver-satile version of the classic UNIX TAR archiver and an innovative method of delivering LZW compressed data over pipes. Portable TAR works with both MS-DOS- and UNIX-compatible machines. Since more than half the source code available from the Internet appears in TAR format, you'll quickly find this a valuable utility. Portable TAR reads and writes archives in ordinary files, raw floppies, and QIC-02 streamer tapes. It understands regular TAR formats, PKZIP, gzip, and UNIX "compress."

Portable TAR has several other advantages over most public-domain TAR programs and those included with UNIX compatible operating systems. Among these advantages are that it:

- processes uniformly under both MS-DOS and UNIX clones;
- reads/writes UNIX-compatible floppies and quarter-inch streamer cartridges under DOS;
- supports unusual floppy formats, such as 80-tracks-by-9-sectors and DEC Rainbow (under DOS);
- has a data compression option under both DOS and UNIX;
- allows you to read System V and/or GNU multivolume archives under DOS and all UNIX clones; and
- includes an option to restore damaged archives, and many other useful options.

As mentioned earlier, Shaporev claims source compatability with most UNIX systems and MS-DOS. Specifically, he provides two makefiles that cover most UNIX implementations and another makefile for Borland Turbo C in MS-DOS. As you might expect, a small amount of assembly language code is provided for supporting functionality not normally found in MS-DOS.

The CUG Library volume of Portable TAR includes binaries built for MS-DOS. Portable TAR v3.15 (as released on 04/05/94) is available as part of CUG #425.

CUG 425B   LZPIPE: Compression Through a Pipe

Shaporev's other contribution is the LZPIPE library, which implements the two most popular compression methods: LZW and "deflate." Both of these methods are de-facto lossless compression standards. LZW is used in the well-known compress utility and deflate is used by number of utilities starting from PKZIP by PKWare Inc. up to the GNU gzip utility.

LZPIPE gives a programming capability analogous to UNIX pipes for systems such as MS-DOS. It also allows access to compressed files. LZPIPE provides a far simpler API than most compression utilities. Specifically, this library processes compressed data in the familiar file handle style of open(), read(), write(), and close() calls.

LZIPE implements only pure compression; no attempt is made to emulate ZIP directory services. Thus, you would either use LZPIPE to compress one file at a time or else add the extra functionality for multi-file archiving yourself.

Source codes for both LZW compression and decompression are derived from sources of compress utility, initially written by Joe Orost. Source codes for deflate compression and inflate decompression are derived from Info-Zip zip/unzip utilities sources. Inflate decompressor was initially written by Mark Adler, and deflate compressor was initially written by Jean-Loup Gailly.

The CUG Library volume of LZIPE includes only C source code. As this is strictly a library, no MS-DOS binaries are included. LZPIPE v1.01 (as released 04/05/94) is available as part of CUG #425.

CUG 426   LPC-Parcor-Cepstrum Code Generator

Patrick Ko Shu Pui (Tai Po, Hong Kong) submits his LPC-Parcor-Cepstrum code generator for C. The LPC-Parcor-Cepstrum code generator (hereafter LPC) can be built on most UNIX platforms as well as Microsoft C/C++ 7.0 and Borland Turbo C v2.0. The primary use of this archive is the manipulation and normalization of audio data files. Specifically, it supports 8-bit ulaw (SUN Sparc), 8-bit and 16-bit PCM data. It then generates LPC autocorrelation or covariance coefficients, Parcor (partial correlation) coefficients, or LPC cepstrum coefficients.

The implementation of LPC draws from algorithms and methods described by Shuzo Saito and Kazuo Nakata in *Fundamentals of Speech Signal Processing* (Academic Press, 1986) and others.

Patrick Ko also contributed the Small Matrix Toolbox (CUG #403). In fact, the LPC application includes several key components from the Small Matrix Toolbox.

The C source package included in LPC is free for academic purposes only. For commercial usage, you must send a a US$30 money order to the address to the author (Patrick Ko). The CUG Library volume includes full C source and binaries for MS-DOS. LPC version 0.52 (as released 04/16/94) is available as CUG #426.

CUG 427   Multijoy: Multi Joystick Interface

Christof Ruch (Clausthal, Germany) submits the Multi Joystick Interface package. This package makes it possible to connect up to six digital joysticks (Atari type) to the parallel port of your PC. For test (or two-player gaming) purposes, two joysticks can be emulated by the keyboard, so you can try out the games before you actually decide to build an interface. Specifically, this archive includes instructions for building the interface, test programs for checking your interface, and Pascal and C interface routines. Several arcade-type games are already publicly available for this system, though none are included with the CUG archive.

As you may recall, the original IBM PC offered analog joystick ports on an optional interface card.[1] This joystick adapter had a fixed I/O address and could support only two joysticks on the PC. Furthermore, the polling of analog joysticks requires a considerable amount of wall-clock time because you must wait for the Resitance/Capacitance (R/C) circuit to dissipate after each poll. The older digital joysticks offer less resolution (only eight possible direction indicators), but can be read with greater speed and precision. The C version of Multi Joystick Interface works specifically with Borland C++ 3.1. The Pascal version works with Borland Turbo Pascal. The code should be portable to other platforms and uses only a few lines of inline assembler code.

Please note that the construction of the hardware interface requires you to etch your own printed circuit board (PCB). Fortunately, the archive includes a PCB layout in postscript, HP PCL, and PCX file formats. And, of course, you'll need to do some soldering to pull it all together. The interface does require power, which can be supplied from your spare analog joystick port (+5VDC, GND) or from an inexpensive wall-type transformer. Ruch estimates the total cost of hardware to be about $30. Hardware construction instructions appear in both English and German.

The Multi Joystick Interface hardware documentation and software development kit are not public domain but are copyrighted by Christof and Henning Ruch. However, it is free software and information. You may use it for whatever you wish, even using it to write public domain, freeware, shareware, and commercial software. You may not, however, re-distribute modified versions of the source code, the executables, and

---

1. Volkman, Victor R. "Complete Joystick Interface." *The C Gazette*, Vol. 5, No. 1, Autumn 1990, pp. 8–21.

the documentation files. The Multi Joystick Interface v1.1 (as released on 03/24/94) is available as CUG #427.

Support Resources

WWW: `ftp://ftp.tu-clausthal.de/pub/msdos/games/multijoy/`

CUG 428   PICTOR: Text-Mode Video Library

Jonathan Wood (Irvine, CA) contributes the PICTOR text-mode video library. PICTOR is a C callable library for MS-DOS development that provides multi-pane stacked windows, pulldown menus, and hypertext help. PICTOR is more than just video: it also includes interrupt-driven serial communications, Ctrl-C and critical error handler, on-screen clock, text compression, and even a sample text editor. The library provides many high-level routines, most of which can easily be implemented in just one or two function calls. For example, the Ctrl-C, Ctrl-Break, and critical error handlers are all installed (and will all uninstall automatically) with a single function call. The library also provides many low-level functions that provide support for custom routines that you create.

This package includes two sets of libraries: one for Microsoft C/ C++ and another for Borland C 3.0. Wherever practical, the library routines are ANSI C compatible; therefore, the library will link with programs compiled with C compilers from most other vendors with little or no modifications.

You may incorporate any of the copyrighted object code in executable form into your own programs, and you may use and distribute these programs royalty-free, provided you include a copyright notice and that your product is substantially different from the library itself. Full licensing information is included with the archive. The PICTOR video library v1.51 (as released on 03/15/94) is available as CUG #428.

CUG 429   Chess for C++, Fastclok, and KBFake

This volume combines three relatively small but powerful archives. Walter Karas (Cary, NC) submits C++ source code for a simple MS-DOS chess game. Walter Karas also contributed the SORTLIST AVL algorithms on CUG #395. Russell Taylor (University of North Carolina at Chapel Hill) contributes archives for redirecting serial I/O and accelerating the PC hardware clock.

CUG 429A   Chess for C++

The Chess for C++ game is very flexible in configuring both human and computer opponents. You can select either human or computer for both black and white playing sides. Thus, you can start a game with zero, one, or two human players. You can assign one of three skill levels to each computer opponent. The number of moves of look-ahead is two for skill level 1, three for skill level 2, and four for skill level 3.

The program display is plain ASCII text, so you might find it a little challenging to get used to (a white pawn is represented by "PW," for example). This should allow it to be ported somewhat easily to other platforms.

Chess for C++ is provided in source code format only, so you must have a C++ compiler installed to use it. Chess for C++ v1.2 (as released on 05/04/94) can be found on volume CUG #432.

CUG 429B   Fastclok and KBFake

Fastclok implements a more precise time than that provided by DOS. Specifically, it provides functions to increase the clock rate to around 1165 interrupts per second. This yields a granularity of 858 microseconds between clock pulses rather than the 55 milliseconds between normal PC clock pulses (18.2 times/second). Under the influence of Fastclok, the gettimeofday() routine acts like the UNIX version, with the exception that time zone does not matter. The time is returned in timeval structures that match their UNIX counterparts.

The start_fasttimer() routine must be called before the gettimeofday() routines will work and the stop_fasttimer() routine *must* be called before the program terminates or a crash will result. For this reason, start_fasttimer() installs the stop_fasttimer() routine to be called at program exit.

Fastclok is implemented entirely in C with the exception of inline assembly language to execute the CLear Interrupt enable (CLI) and Set InTerrupt enable (STI) instructions. Only source code is provided for these routines, so you must have a C compiler available to use them.

KBFake is a terminate and stay resident (TSR) program that redirects the input from one serial line so that incoming characters appear to have been typed on the keyboard. It works by installing an interrupt handler for the serial port that is to be used. This handler inserts the characters coming in over the serial line into the keyboard buffer using the BIOS keyboard write call.

The code for this program is a mixture of the example for the keep( ) function call in Borland C and various programming examples from the SIMTEL internet FTP site. The keep( ) function call does not have a direct replacement in Microsoft C/C++.

This is an interrupt service routine. Accordingly, you *must* compile it with Test Stack Overflow disabled to get an executable file that will operate correctly. The CUG volume of KBFake includes both C source and an MS-DOS executable.

CUG 430   M68kdis: Motorola M68000 through M68030 Disassembler

Christopher G. Phillips (University of Texas at Austin) submits his m68kdis disassembler for the Motorola 68000 family of CPU chips. Disassemblers are system software that accept a binary executable as input and produce assembly language source as output. Specifically, m68kdis supports the full instruction sets of the 68000, 68008, 68010, 68020, and 68030 CPU chips. Additionally, m68kdis decodes instructions for the 68851 Paged Memory Unit and the 68881/68882 Floating-Point Coprocessors. The Motorola 68000 family chips power millions of computers, including the Macintosh, Atari, Amiga, and many embedded CPU industrial applications. The CUG Library edition of m68kdis includes full source in C (no executables are provided). The m68kdis disassembler is available as CUG volume #441. Since m68kdis is portable, it is actually a cross-disassembler. For example, you can disassemble 68000 programs on a variety of host CPUs from PCs to UNIX machines. Phillips provides a very clean makefile without any OS-specific flags or options. He also takes care to avoid common pitfalls such as dependencies on the size of the int data type.

CUG 431   DOSRIFS: Share Hard Disk or CD-ROM Drives

Kyle A. York (McGraw-Hill School Systems) submits his Remote Installable File System for DOS. The Remote Installable File System provides a LAN linking two computers through the serial port so they may share resources. RIFS installs itself as a TSR using the MSCDEX convention for installable file systems. Shareable resources are currently limited to available disk drives including hard disks, CD-ROM, and network drives. RIFS also supports the redirection of a client parallel port to a file or device on the server. RIFS supplies 32-bit cyclic redundancy check (CRC) to guarantee error-free file transfers.

The CUG Library volume includes full source in C and ASM as well as MS-DOS executables. RIFS for DOS (released 10/08/94) is available as CUG volume #431.

CUG 432   PTMID and WildFile

CUG 432A   PTMID: MIDI/MOD Converter

Andrew Scott (Mosman Park, Australia) submits his PTMID music conversion utility. Specifically, PTMID takes general MIDI files (format 0 or 1) and converts them to Protracker MOD files or Multitracker MTM files. As you may know, MIDI files are industry standard, but need some sort of sequencer to be played. This is because there can be near-infinite simultaneous notes present (though about 20 is a standard maximum). Protracker files are four-channel files (though six, eight, or more channels can be supported), but have a bank of digitized instruments included. This allows sound of a reasonable quality to be produced with limited hardware. Multitracker files are similar to MOD files and support up to 32 simultaneous notes. PTMID v0.3 (released on 07/18/94) is available as CUG Library volume #432A.

The CUG Library volume includes a MS-DOS executable as well as complete source code in ANSI C. The source can be recompiled using Borland C 2.0 (or later). The makefile builds a small memory model program, though other models may be possible. The documentation appears in the form of a six-page UNIX man file. Some background in digital music is a prerequisite to getting the best results from the code. PTMID is distributed with a license reminiscent of the GNU Public License. Specifically, you may not resell the program, all redistributions must include PTMID source, and anything built using the PTMID source must include a notice that parts are derived from it.

CUG 432B   WildFile: Shell-Style Wildcard Filename

John Kercheval (Seattle, WA) contributes his WildFile library that provides UNIX shell style wildcarding in MS-DOS executables. Wildcarding means the ability to take a description such as foo*.c and return a list of matching filenames (e.g., foobar.c, foofoo.c, etc.). By default, MS-DOS programs can accept the support for arbitrary string (*) and single character (?) wildcarding if they use the INT 21h service functions FindFirst and FindNext. WildFile starts with this level of support and adds on regular expressions using pattern primitives such

as positive closure (+), character range ([ ]), and character negation (!
or ^). WildFile v1.20 (as released on 01/07/92) is available as CUG Library volume #432B.

Here are some examples of legal WildFile expressions and results:

Expression	Result
t	would match to the filenames test.doc, wet.goo, itsy.bib, foo.tic, etc.
th?[a-eg]	would match to any file without an extension, the two letters of which were th, with any third letter and the last letter of which was a, b, c, d, e, or g (i.e., thug, thod, thud, etc.).
*	would match all filenames.
f[!a-l]o*	would match foo*.* but not fao*.* through flo*.*

WildFile documentation consists mainly of a series of concatenated release notes for v1.00 through1.20. WildFile has been developed and compiled using both MicroSoft C v6.00A and Borland C++ 2.00. Kercheval has generously dedicated WildFile to the public domain.

CUG 433   SVGACC: MS-DOS Graphics Library

Stephen L. Balkum and Daniel A. Sill (Zephyr Software, Austin, TX) submit their MS-DOS real-mode SVGA graphics library for MSC, Borland C, and Symantec C/C++. SVGACC provides an easy interface to the high-resolution/high-color video modes of the newer SVGA video cards. There has been no standard for VGA video cards above the 320x200x256 resolution. Instead, each video card manufacturer has implemented a slightly different method to access these high-resolution/high-color video modes. SVGACC automatically identifies the video card and its installed memory. Users may write graphics programs that will work on most any SVGA card without writing specific versions for each individual SVGA card. Over 100 functions support sprite animation, drawing primitives, fills, 3-D views, and much more. SVGACC is written in 100 percent assembly language and uses 80386 32-bit registers for the best possible speed. SVGACC v2.1 (as released on 05/09/94) is available as CUG volume #433.

SVGACC specifically supports the following SuperVGA graphics cards:

Acumos	NCR
Avance Logic	Oak Technologies
ATI Technologies	Realtek
Ahead	Paradise/Western Digital
Chips and Technologies	Primus
CirrusLogic	Trident
Everex Micro Enhancer	Tseng Labs
Genoa	Video 7
Mxic	

All VESA-compatible SuperVGAs (v1.00 and greater)

The maximum resolution available depends on the video card, its installed memory, and monitor. Most VGA video cards support the 320x200x256 and 640x400x256 video modes. 512Kb of video memory is required. To support the 640x480x256 and 800x600x256 video modes. One Mb of video memory is required to support the 1024x768x256 video mode. Two Mb of video memory is required to support the 1280x1024x256 video mode.

The SVGACC documentation consists of its comprehensive Reference Manual (270 pages). The Reference Manual primarily provides detailed descriptions of each of the more than 100 SVGACC library functions. Each entry includes a function prototype, descriptions of input and output parameters, usage notes, see-also, and detailed example code fragments. An appendix provides complete wiring schematics for standard PC analog joystick ports.

Since SVGACC is marketed as shareware, you must register with Zephyr Software after a 30-day evaluation period. Registration is only $35 for the first copy and $5 for upgrades. Registration entitles you to unlimited runtime distribution rights. Registered users also receive several other benefits:

- extra functions, including GIF and XMS support and convex polygon fills;
- documentation in WinWord 2.0 format;
- font editor and font object files;
- mouse cursor editor;

- limited telephone technical support; and
- discounts on upgrades and alternative DOS versions.

Source code for SVGACC is not available in any release.

CUG 434   XYZ++ 3-D Graphics

Nicholas Centanni (Los Gatos, CA) submits his 3-D graphics class library for Borland C++ 3.1 (and later). XYZ++ is a comprehensive package of optimized C++ classes for both floating-point and fixed-point 3-D graphics.

XYZ++ is shipped with the following 3-D mathematics classes:

Class	Description
Viewer	Performs all 3-D calculations to define a scene.
Vect	A small vector mathematics class used by both the Viewer and Light classes.
d_Light	A surface shading calculator (double values).
f_Light	A surface shading calculator (fixed point).

In addition, the DOS BGI programs use their own group of classes:

Class	Description
Graphics	A BGI-specific high-level graphics class.
Panel	Classes for building GUI control panels.
Mouse	A complete graphical mouse support class.
Keyboard	An extended-keyboard support class.
Timer	A simple high-resolution timer class.
Scene	A demonstration of packaging XYZ++ with the supplied Graphics class.

XYZ++ v2.0 object code (as released on 07/21/94) is available as CUG volume #434. The XYZ++ package is divided into two distinct segments. The first is a group of classes that perform only 3-D mathematics, without reference to, or dependence on, any specific method of graphics output. The second deals with the output and display of graphics using Borland's BGI drivers, but without any specific reference to 3-D mathematics.

The system is segmented in this way in order to allow developers to replace the supplied graphics classes cleanly with those of their own, without disturbing the 3-D mathematics functionality of the package. The system can then be easily connected to any graphics library or graphics engine that the developer wishes to use.

XYZ++ documentation consists of a 40-page ASCII reference manual. The manual defines and reviews many 3-D concepts, though some additional study may be necessary if this is your first 3-D application. Since XYZ++ is marketed as shareware, you must register with its author after a 30-day evaluation period. Registration is only $47 and entitles you to full source code as well as unlimited run-time distribution rights. Registered users also receive several other benefits:

- latest version of XYZ++ with `makefiles` for other processors and memory models;
- printed manual;
- Virtual Reality demo source, which displays a pyramid above a GUI-navigation control panel, allowing the user to move about in the scene;
- Night Bird demo source which a real-time 3-D graphics animation of a white bird flying endlessly over a colorful field of stars;
- WaterVision animation source which allows you to control up to nine colorful water fountains, where each of hundreds of water drops is individually animated;
- Liberty Bell game source which is a 21-bell nickel slot machine that uses the same symbols arranged in the same order, and calculates winning payoffs the same way as the real machine.

CUG 435   VESATEST: Demos SVGA and .Voc/.Wav Audio

Jason Hughes (Abilene, TX) submits his VESA SVGA graphics demonstration that includes many other programming elements essential to writing MS-DOS games. The graphics demonstrations take you through many fast-moving animations that show off the VESA 640x480x256 color display mode. I was particularly impressed with its speed even on my slow 80386DX-20MHz CPU. Additional graphics routines show off the virtual paging capabilities of SVGAs with more than 1Mb RAM on board. The CUG Library volume of VesaTest includes full source code in Borland C++ v3.1 along with MS-DOS executables. VesaTest v2 (as released on 07/20/94) is available as CUG #435.

In addition to fast graphics, VesaTest includes integrated routines for full digitized sound support. This allows playback of both MS Windows `.wav` and Sound Blaster `.voc` files. The playback routines use double-buffering and DMA/IRQ detection so that configuration is fully automatic.

Also in this package are mouse routines that intercept mouse interrupts with full support for two-button and three-button mice. Two-button users can simulate the middle button by pressing left and right buttons simultaneously. This gives the developer more freedom to use mouse buttons. The latest version also allows automatic mouse acceleration for those mouse drivers that don't yet provide it.

VesaTest does not include any documentation other than a brief explanatory README file. However, the comments in the code should be enough to give you a basic idea of what's happening. Hughes has released VesaTest as "tagware," which means that if you use it then you are asked to put a tag line in your program's title screen. His notes also indicate he would like to receive postcards in lieu of registration fees.

CUG 436   INCON:INput CONtrol Library

Richard Zigler (McBain, MI) submits his INput CONtrol (INCON) library for developing sophisticated data input screens in MS-DOS applications. INCON gives you control over the placement and appearance of input fields, and the type and amount of data that each will accept. Input fields may be alphanumeric, uppercase, integer, or floating-point. The INCON library supports Borland Turbo C v2.01 (or later) and will build compact, small, medium, or large memory model versions. INCON v3.1 (as released on 10/08/94) is available as CUG #436.

You may pass a string to INCON and specify that it be treated as default input, an input template, or both. Templates may be alpha, numeric, or mixed. You may specify that fields scroll, that they be delimited, that user input be hidden, and that input be returned to your program left-or right-justified or centered in a field whose width and "pad" character you select. A number of reserved edit keys give users of your programs extensive input editing capabilities. Several assembly language string-handling routines are available as part of INCON and in a separate object file.

The basic operation of the program is as follows:

1. The calling routine defines a block of parameters, among which is a far pointer to an I/O buffer.

2. At entry, INCON copies any string in the I/O buffer to an internal work buffer and may then display it as default input or use it to construct an input template, or both.
3. User keyboard entries are examined. INCON acts upon its reserved keys immediately. It returns extended-key codes that it finds in a list provided by the calling routine and cancels the input operation. It displays and saves in the work buffer all entries that are appropriate to the field type; it discards all others.
4. If the operation succeeds, INCON copies user input to the I/O buffer, overwriting its previous contents. If it fails or is canceled, INCON discards any user input it has so far gathered.
5. INCON returns a code to the calling routine that indicates input status or whether the user has made a special request.

The INCON documentation consists of a 26-page reference and tutorial manual. The manual appears as an ASCII file formatted out to 66 lines/page. The documentation provides in-depth information on all parameters and data structures you need to use. Additionally, a well-documented demonstration program makes it easy to learn.

Since Zigler has committed INCON to the public domain, there are no fees required for its use. The CUG Library edition includes full source code in C and ASM files. Demonstration MS-DOS executables are also included.

CUG 437   C/C++ Exploration Tools for Windows

C/C++ Exploration Tools for Windows, by Juergen Mueller (Kornwestheim, Germany), includes both his C Function Tree Generator (CFT) and the C Structure Tree Generator (CST). CFT and CST analyse the C/C++ source code of applications of any size with multiple files. CFT and CST are useful to explore new, unknown software and to support re-use, maintenance, and re-engineering. By preprocessing, scanning, and analyzing the program source code, these programs generate the function call hierarchy (CFT) and the data structure/class (CST) relations. Both programs can handle C and C++ code; CFT can also analyze assembler code. The C Exploration Tools for Windows executables (released 09/11/94) are available as CUG volume #437.

The C Exploration Tools are shareware and require registration with the author if you decide to use them beyond the 30-day evaluation period. The registration price is $46 U.S. or 60 DM for a single copy. Generous site license discounts with prices as low as $15 are appropriate for corporate use or educational institutions. Registered users of the

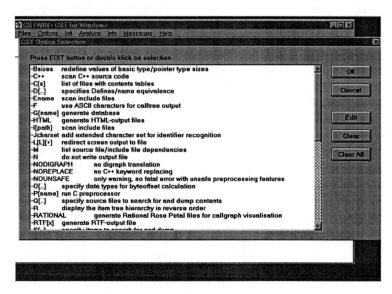

Just a few of the many user-configurable options of C Exploration
Tools for Windows

MS Windows version automatically receive the Win32s version that
can be used with Windows NT or Windows 95. Source code for the C
Exploration Tools is not available.

The C Exploration Tools for Windows v1.04 is functionally identical to the C Exploration Tools for MS-DOS v2.30 (see CUG #391).
However, the Windows version also allows you to configure the in-
creasingly complex set of options via the GUI (see the preceding figure) and also captures textual output in a scrolling window. Please note
that you must register the MS-DOS and Windows versions separately.

CUG 438   STELNET: Serial Telnet for DOS

Riku Saikkonen (Finland) submits his telnet client for MS-DOS,
which uses the serial port as the I/O device. Although designed for
Bulletin Board System (BBS) applications, STELNET works equally
well without any BBS software. STELNET requires a FOSSIL driver
and the Waterloo TCP library. It supports binary mode telnet (8-bit),
and a "8-bit clean mode," in which all 256 characters are cleanly transferred in both directions. STELNET does not do any terminal emulation of its own; it should never change the data transferred (except
where protocol requirements designate).

STELNET conforms to the "conditionally compliant" definition of telnet client as specified in `http://www.cis.ohio-state.edu/htbin/rfc/rfc1123.html` RFC 1123. The telnet code uses the Waterloo TCP library (WATTCP), which uses a packet driver. WATTCP is not included in this volume but is freely available at ftp://`ftp.bhp.com.au/pc/selected/network/wattcp.zip`. Any network adapter with a packet driver should work. SLIP should work, at least with the Ether-SLIP packet driver.

STELNET is distributed under the GNU General Public License, v2, and thus includes source code. Source code is all in C which compiles under Borland C, in either small or large memory models. STELNET v1.00 (released on 12/20/94) is available as CUG #438.

Support Resources

e-mail: `rjs@spider.compart.fi`

CUG 439   XLIB: DOS Extender Library

David Pyles (Jackson, MS) offers his DOS Extender Library for producing Protected Mode MS-DOS applications. XLIB is an assembly language library that greatly simplifies protected-mode programming under Microsoft DOS. With only two calls to XLIB, assembly language programs can utilize the simplicity and power of 32-bit processing. C and C++ programs can harness the powers of 16-bit protected mode using inline assembly. Additionally, the XLIB archive contains a second library call, `EASYX`, which allows all high-level languages to gain access to extended memory.

XLIB is designed for the Intel 386, 486, and Pentium processors. XLIB fully utilizes the 32-bit processing modes of these chips and makes them available to the user. The compactness of XLIB follows largely from the fact that much of it is written in 32-bit code.

XLIB is marketed as shareware and you may evaluate it for up to 30 days. If you want to distribute applications that incorporate XLIB, then you must register it. Registration is $40 for the basic license and an extra $20 if technical support is desired. It includes an extensive 60-page manual in plain ASCII format as well as sample code. XLIB works with either Borland or Microsoft C environments. XLIB v5.1 (released on 08/25/95) is available as CUG #439.

Support Resources

e-mail: `74730.167@compuserve.com`

CUG 440   BESTLibrary of C Functions

George Vanous (Delta, BC) submits his library of essential and efficient C-callable functions. Although oriented toward MS-DOS, many of the algorithms are relevant on other platforms, such as Windows and UNIX. BESTLibrary consists of 282 functions coded in assembler and 68 functions written in C. All calls require far pointers (e.g., large memory model). The library functions are roughly categorized as:

- text and .ini files (18 functions),
- low-level keyboard (42 functions),
- linked list (6 functions),
- math and matrices (26 functions),
- 2-D and 3-D vectors (33 functions),
- mouse (13 functions),
- string manipulation (80 functions),
- text-mode screen I/0 (60 functions),
- SVGA bitmaps with animation (50 functions), and
- much more!

BESTLibrary is freeware, but the author would like to hear all comments from users of the library (email or postcards). The CUG Library volume includes code for the 68 functions with C source. For the source to the assembly language portion, you must register with the author for a nominal fee of $10. BESTLibrary v2.32 (released 09/12/94) is available as CUG #440.

Support Resources

e-mail: vanous@helix.net

CUG 441   VGA Editor with Animation

George Vanous (Delta, BC) also submits his VGA Editor for editing and animating graphics images with full mouse support. The VGA Editor creates graphics files that are fully portable into C and Pascal programs in conjunction with BESTLibrary (CUG #440). The editor is ideal for drawing small pictures and animations for use with 16-color VGA modes. VGA Editor will also read in Windows .ico files for editing (but does not yet support writing them). The editor can accomodate multiple-frame animations in a single editing session. The following figure shows the zoom style of editing on a single frame.

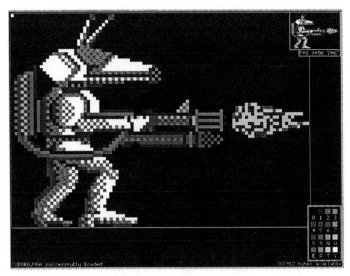

Zoom style editing on a single animation frame

VGA Editor is distributed as shareware and you must register the product if you find it worthy of continued use. Registration is only $5 and includes complete documentation on the operation of VGA Editor and integrating graphics into your programs. The complete C source code for VGA Editor is also available for $10.

Support Resources

e-mail: vanous@helix.net

CUG 442   C Pointer and Array Tutorial

Ted Jensen (Redwood City, CA) has contributed his manuscript "A Tutorial on Pointers and Arrays in C" to help novice C programmers learn proper usage of these critical language elements. I still have vivid memories of my trials with pointers during my own apprenticeship in C more than 10 years ago. Jensen's work is based on a tutorial originally found in Bob Stout's popular "SNIPPETS" C code collection.

Jensen provides 10 chapters of tutorial information as listed below, that is profusely illustrated with detailed source code.

- What Is a Pointer?
- Pointer Types and Arrays

- Pointers and Strings
- More on Strings
- Pointers and Structures
- More on Strings and Arrays of Strings
- More on Multi-Dimensional Arrays
- Pointers to Arrays
- Pointers and Dynamic Allocation of Memory
- Pointers to Functions

Version 0.2 of the tutorial (released 12/19/95) is available as CUG #442.

Support Resources

e-mail: tjensen@netcom.com

CUG 443   CNCL: Communication Networks Class Library

Martin Steppler (Aachen University of Technology, Germany) submits the Communication Networks Class Library (CNCL), a C++ library created by the Communication Networks Department of Aachen. CNCL is both a class library featuring generic C++ classes and a simulation library with strong points in random number generation, statistics, and event-driven simulation.

- Generic classes
  - Tree-structured class hierarchy, similar to NIH class lib
  - General-purpose classes (e.g., arrays, linked lists, AVL trees)
  - Interface classes for UNIX system calls: pipes, select, sockets
  - Persistent objects
- Simulation
  - Event-driven simulation classes
  - Statistical evaluation classes
  - Random number generator and distribution classes
- Fuzzy logic
  - Fuzzy sets, fuzzy variables, fuzzy rules and inference engine for building fuzzy controllers and expert systems
  - Fuzzy rules to C++ translator
- Graphics
  - Interface classes for DEC's ezd graphics server
  - Interface classes for GIST graphics server (available separately)

CNCL is distributed under the GNU General Public License, v2, and thus includes source code. Although the graphics require DEC Ultrix, the remaining classes should work fine with any GNU-compatible C++ compiler. PC users *must* obtain WinZip or a similar utility to unpack the files, which are Tarred and Zipped (.tz). CNCL v1.4 (released 01/05/96) is available as CUG #443.

Support Resources

e-mail: `cncl-adm@comnets.rwth-aachen.de`
WWW: `http://www.comnets.rwth-aachen.de/doc/cncl.html`

CUG 444 Mendel's Games

Mendel Cooper (Grantsville, MD) contributes a volume of MS-DOS games: Wordy, ChessClock, and Chaos Game. Wordy is an educational word-game study system that builds pattern and word recognition skills used in Scrabble™ and Boggle™. The Wordy practice game checks words you unscramble against a 100,000 word dictionary. Wordy also includes standalone `Search`, `Anagram`, `UnScramble`, and word-pattern find utilities. A `BINGO` utility looks up all valid permutations of letters of a word. The `1DIF` utility finds all legal words constructed by substituting a single letter. WORDY received a five-star (highest possible) rating in *PC Computing* (December 1995, p. 365).

ChessClock includes a digital display, move counter, pause function, and more. It requires VGA and 386 or better to run. Its also useful for timing Scrabble ™ games because the clocks may be paused.

One of the discoveries of the new science of Chaos is that there seems to be an underlying order in randomness. The Chaos Game uses the Sierpinsky Gasket, a figure with a fractal dimension of less than two. Requires VGA and 386 or better to run.

The CUG Library edition includes full Borland C/C++ source code for each program. Each of Mendel's programs is shareware, with an extremely low registration fee (less than $5) for each program. Mendel's Games (released 12/22/95) is available as CUG #444.

Support Resources

e-mail: `thegrendel@theriver.com`
         `thegrendel@aol.com`
WWW: `http://personal.riverusers.com/~thegrendel`

CUG 445   Mendel's Utilities

Mendel's second volume includes an eclectic mixture of 10 different text and graphics utility and algorithm demonstrations. Here's a list of what you'll find:

- Countdown timer — for use with board games, cooking, and other applications.
- Alert — combination burglar alarm and screen saver. It flashes a warning message on the screen and simulates a phone dialing the police.
- OneTime — an extremely secure file encryption system based on the one-time cipher used by intelligence agencies.
- Butterfly — colorful graphic demonstration of Pikover's butterfly curves.
- CountUp — restartable count-up timer with a very large digital display.
- Pi5Ways — demonstrates calculating the value of PI in five different ways.
- WCHILL — wind-chill calculator.
- Fractional calculator and fraction class (C++).
- Soundex: — algorithm for translating names into a form suitable for archiving.
- Blank — a simple-minded screen saver.

The CUG Library edition includes full Borland C/C++ source code for each program. Each of Mendel's programs is shareware with an extremely low registration fee (less than $5) for each program. Mendel's Utilities (released 12/22/95) is available as CUG #445.

Support Resources

e-mail: `thegrendel@theriver.com`
             `thegrendel@aol.com`
WWW: `http://personal.riverusers.com/~thegrendel`

CUG 446   Diffpack Solves PDEs

Are Magnus Bruaset and Hans Petter Langtangen of the SINTEF group at the University of Oslo (Norway) submit Diffpack, a fully object oriented framework in C++ for solution of partial differential equations (PDEs). PDEs often arise in the mathematical modeling of physical processes involving, for example, fluid mechanics or waves.

Some typical uses of Diffpack include standard model PDEs, 3-D linear wave equation, incompressible Navier-Stokes, and stochastic ODEs. Diffpack can interface with gnuPlot and plotmtv. You can even construct MPEG movies from multiple visualization frames.

Diffpack has been certified to run in any of the following environments: Hewlett Packard HP-UX 9.05 and C++ 3.50, Silicon Graphics IRIX 5.2 and C++ 3.2.1, Sun Sparc Solaris 2.3/SunOS 5.3 and C++ 4.0. Diffpack v1.4 is available as CUG #446.

Support Resources

e-mail: hpl@math.uio.no

Are.Magnus.Bruaset@si.sintef.no

WWW: http://www.oslo.sintef.no/avd/33/3340/diffpack/

CUG 447   RELAY: Design and Coordinate Overload Protection Devices

Michael F. Watson and Dean Lance Smith contribute RELAY: an interactive overload protection design tool for electrical engineers. Relay plots the time-current characteristics of overcurrent protection devices and coordinates the overcurrent protection devices at an electric distribution substation. The source code is entirely in C and includes makefiles for the Microsoft C compiler. The RELAY.EXE executable requires MS-DOS and VGA display.

The traditional approach to staging overcurrent protection devices has been to plot the time-current curves for various relay settings using paper and pencil, compare the curves of the various relays and fuses, and then adjust the settings of the relays until a solution is reached. RELAY reduces the time required to complete the task and provides greater accuracy. Relay v1.0 is available on CUG CD-ROM as volume #447.

Support Resources

e-mail: dsmith@scs.howard.edu

CUG 448   Automatic Computer Troubleshooting with Signature Analysis

Surojit Chatterjee and Dean Lance Smith submit a tool for detecting digital circuit problems via signature analysis. Signature analysis is a technique used in servicing microprocessor-based systems. With this technique, an instrument called a "signature analyzer" is used to check a digital circuit by detecting the bit streams at various nodes of the circuit. The bit streams are displayed as hexadecimal signatures. The actual signature of a node is compared with its predetermined correct signature. The result of the comparison is used to trace faults in the system down to the component level. This volume includes complete source in C and MS-DOS executables. The source supports Borland Turbo C but could possibly be ported to other environments. Signature analysis v1.0 is available on CUG CD-ROM as volume #448.

Support Resources

e-mail: dsmith@scs.howard.edu

CUG 449   NULLSOCK: Allows Offline Use of Winsock Applications

Nullsock, by Jean-Michel Mercier (Paris, France), is a Winsock simulator that allows you to run Winsock applications offline. This is most useful for forcing a web browser to work on offline copies of HTML files that you have downloaded. You might want to do this because you're "on the road" with a portable computer but without an immediate Internet connection, or perhaps to avoid paying online charges to view material you've already downloaded several times. Nullsock works by loading a dummy WINSOCK.DLL with its entry points replaced by stubs. You can either run Nullsock directly or use Nullsock to spawn the desired application. Nullsock was designed to work with Windows 3.11 and has been tested with Netscape and AIR Mosaic. It will work with Windows 95, but only when running 16-bit Winsock applications. Nullsock includes complete C source and compiles with Borland C. Nullsock v1.0 is available on CUG CD-ROM as volume #449.

Support Resources

e-mail: 100101.1152@compuserve.COM

CUG 450   CppIma: A C++ Image Processing Class Library

Klamer Schutte of the TNO Physics and Electronics Laboratory (The Hague, Netherlands) contributes the CppIma image-processing class library. CppIma library provides an interface to common operations on images for C++ applications. The operations include file I/O, image creation, iterators for traversing images, and histogram creation.

The library enables easy construction of image processing programs. Secondarily, Schutte hopes to achieve reasonable performance and create an image library independent API. CppIma achieves the latter by its support for three popular base libraries:

- ima(3) — a simplified version of the image library from the University of Twente, The Netherlands, is included with CppIma.
- Khoros — a tool for information processing and visualization with an extensive image processing library (http://www-spires. slac.stanford.edu/FIND/FREEHEP/NAME/KHOROS/FULL)
- Scil-Image — a large collection of linear filters, morphologic filters, segmentation algorithms, measurement functions and arithmetic operations for both 2-D and 3-D binary, gray, floating point, complex-valued, and color images.

CpplIma works with the GNU C++ compiler (g++) and most Cfront-based compilers. It requires 32-bit integer and 64-bit doubles. CpplIma is distributed under terms of the GNU Public License, v2. It is available on the CUG CD-ROM as volume #450.

Support Resources

e-mail: klamer@ph.tn.tudelft.nl
WWW: http://www.ph.tn.tudelft.nl/~klamer/Klamer.html

CUG 451   ClipPloy: Polygon Clipping with Set Operators

Schutte has also contributed ClipPoly, an extended C++ polygon clipping library with set operators. Classical clipping algorithms will tell you whether a point x is within a given polygonA. ClipPoly handles the more general case of two polygons A and B where you want to know the areas of intersection of A and B, A minus B, and B minus A. Although the Weiler-Atherton algorithm already solves this case, Schutte presents a simpler but just as effective algorithm. The ClipPoly algorithm requires only that all polygons are non-self-intersecting (i.e., there are no holes).

ClipPoly requires a C++ compiler with template support, such as GNU C++ v2.6.3 or later. The algorithm is primarily supported on SUN and SGI UNIX platforms, though other platforms may also work. ClipPoly is distributed under terms of the GNU Public License, v2. It is available on the CUG CD-ROM as volume #451.

Support Resources

e-mail: klamer@ph.tn.tudelft.nl
WWW: http://www.ph.tn.tudelft.nl/~klamer/Klamer.html

CUG 452 Freedock: Windows App Manager with Source

Sean Gordon (Fife, Scotland) submits Freedock, a Windows "dock" program that includes the full source code in C. A dock is kind of a miniature version of Program Manager that holds icons for the small number of applications that you use most often. Freedock also remembers your preferred window geometry for each application that you register with it. This saves you from the burden of re-arranging your windows each time you startup an application. A "previewer" allows you to check or change the window geometry without actually launching the applications. The entire dock can be scaled in a way similar to the MS Office Manager dock.

Freedock includes compiled versions of a Win16 executable for Windows 3.1 (FREEDK16.EXE) and a Win32 executable for Windows 95 and NT (FREEDK32.EXE). The Freedock archive includes source code written in C for use with Borland C/C++ or Microsoft Visual C/C++ v1.5 (16-bit) and v2.0 (32-bit). In the Win32 version, you can choose to start applications in separate memory. Freedock is freeware and any programs derived from its source must remain freeware. Freedock v2.5 is available on the CUG CD-ROM as volume #452.

Support Resources

e-mail: sean.gordon@dundee.attgis.com

CUG 453 MetaKit: Persistent Storage of Structured C++ Objects

Jean-Claude Wippler (Houten, Netherlands) contributes his MetaKit, a compact class library for data storage and easy manipulation of structured objects and collections in C++. MetaKit works with any C++ compiler that supports Microsoft Foundation Classes including VC++, Borland C++, and Symantec C++. MetaKit allows your data to be loaded on demand, which allows you access to any size files. It uses traditional database metaphors of begin work/commit work/rollback work with automatic file storage allocation and reclamation. MetaKit allows data to be "flattened" for efficient streaming over sockets and pipes. It encapsulates data in terms of view, row, and property classes. Data can be conveniently accessed via "[]" and "( )" by operator overloading. Applications can statically link MetaKit or load it as a DLL.

MetaKit is distributed as shareware. If you use it beyond the 30-day evaluation period then you must register it. Personal-use registration is $25 and commercial-use registration is $65 (includes full source code).

The evaluation copy of MetaKit v1.2 is available on the CUG CD-ROM as volume #453.

Support Resources

e-mail: `jcw@meta4.nl`
WWW: `http://www.meta4.com/meta4/`

CUG 454   SWMP: Sound Wizards Module Player

Beat Rigazzi (Oberonz, Switzerland) submits the Sound Wizards Module Player (SWMP), a driver for playing .mod sound files through any digital audio card (SoundBlaster compatible). The .mod audio file format is a multichannel sampled audio file that supports four, six, or eight simultaneous channels. The .mod file has fewer limitations than the .wav file and for that reason has become widely used by electronic music and game producers. SWMP includes several example .mod tracks for you to experiment with, and a standalone MS-DOS player program (*SWMP.EXE*). SWMP provides an API and calling interfaces for Borland C/C++, Assembler, and Pascal. You can integrate the library simply by including the header file and linking in MOD_DRV.OBJ (source not provided).

The driver has a small API, but you can start your first MOD file playing with as few as three function calls. A powerful hardware detection identifies configurations of Sound Blaster, SoundBlaster Pro, and Gravis UltraSound digital audio adapters. This lets users avoid having to remember obscure DMA and I/O port settings. SWMP is freeware and can be incorporated into other freeware programs. If you want to use SWMP in a commercial product, you must contact the author first. SWMP v1.41 is available on the CUG CD-ROM as volume #454.

Support Resources

e-mail: `rigazzi@iamexwi.unibe.ch`

CUG 455   Advanced I/O C++ Class Library

Oleg Kiselyov (Denton, TX) offers his Advanced I/O C++ Class Library, which enhances the capabilities of stream I/O with encoding and compression. Some of these features include:

- filenames with pipes embedded;
- explicit Endian I/O of short/long integers (guarantees portability);

- stream sharing of different I/O types;
- simple variable-length coding of short integers; and
- arithmetic compression of a stream of integers.

The Advanced I/O Class Library has been designed with portability in mind: it compiles on UNIX (GNU C++), Macintosh, and MS-DOS platforms (including Borland C++). Kiselyov has placed this library in the public domain. Advanced I/O library v2.23 is available on the CUG CD-ROM as volume #455.

Support Resources

e-mail: oleg@pobox.com
         oleg@acm.org
WWW: http://pobox.com/~oleg/ftp/
         http://pobox.com/~oleg/ftp/packages/

CUG 456   LZHLIB: LZH Data Compression Library

Kerwin F. Medina (New Westminster, BC) contributes LZHLIB, a small C library with the minimum code neccessary to compress and uncompress using the LZH algorithm. This library is a direct derivative of the source code of Haruhiko Okumura's popular ar archiver. Medina has created the library so an application can make use of compression with a function call and without having to spawn an external compression program. The library has only two API functions: lzh_freeze (to compress) and lzh_melt (to decompress). In both cases, the caller has only to provide the I/O functions and memory allocation functions. The interface is simple enough that you can integrate it with fewer than 20 additional lines of code in your program. LZHLIB can be built on MS-DOS, UNIX, and other platforms. LZHLIB as released on 04/18/96 is available on the CUG CD-ROM as volume #456.

Support Resources

e-mail: kerwin@infoserve.net
WWW: ftp://ftp.elf.stuba.sk/pub/pc/pack/

CUG 457 dmalloc: Debug Memory Allocation Library

Gray Watson (Pittsburgh, PA) submits dmalloc, the debug memory allocation library. The dmalloc library has been designed as a drop-in replacement for C run-time malloc(), realloc(), calloc(), free(), and other memory management routines. It provides many debugging facilities that you can configure at run-time, including memory-leak tracking, fence-post write detection, file/line number reporting, and general logging of statistics.

dmalloc is highly portable and users report success on many platforms, including AIX, BSDI, DG/UX, HPUX, Irix, Linux, MS-DOS, NeXT, OSF, Solaris, SunOS, Ultrix, Unixware, and Cray Y-MP. The package includes the library, configuration scripts, debug utility application, test program, and docs (ASCII and PostScript). dmalloc is free for academic and non-commercial use. Commercial users must register as shareware for U.S. $35. dmalloc v3.2.1 as released on 9/30/95 is available on the CUG CD-ROM as volume #457.

Support Resources

e-mail: gray@letters.com
WWW: http://www.digits.com/dmalloc/
FTP: ftp://ftp.letters.com

CUG 458 Grayimage: Grayscale Image C++ Class Library

Oleg Kiselyov (Denton, TX) contributes Grayimage, a C++ class library for dealing with full-depth grayscale images. Grayimage supports all standard image algebra/arithmetics, including dealing with image slices, histogram equalization, and computing various norms and scalar products. The package reads and writes PGM, XWD, and Group G (grayscale) TIFF file formats with automatic recognition of the input image file format. It's possible to assign one image to another to fit, no matter what their dimensions are.

Grayimage is highly portable: Oleg has personally verified ports for UNIX with GNU C++ (SUN, HP-UX), Macintosh with Metrowerk's C++, and Windows 95 and NT with Borland C++. Grayimage v2.2.3 as released on 03/31/96 is available as volume #458.

Support Resources

e-mail: oleg@pobox.com
       oleg@acm.org
WWW: http://pobox.com/~oleg/ftp/
       http://pobox.com/~oleg/ftp/packages/

CUG 459   MasterMind: C++ Game Pits Man Against Computer

Alex Hunger (Adlington, Lancashire UK) submits MMND, a game that puts the computer in the role of "codebreaker" in the classic MasterMind™ boardgame. The interesting aspect of Hunger's implementation is that the computer can guess a pattern that you choose. It uses an optimal information-theoretic algorithm and so plays extraordinarily well — better than any human being. This takes a lot of computation, so patterns chosen are stored in a data file so a computation never needs to be made twice. The patterns chosen are put through a randomizing algorithm that makes the game more interesting to play, without losing optimality.

MMND is written in C++ and should compile under any C++ compiler with multiple inheritance, ANSI header files, and ANSI libraries. This includes MS-DOS and UNIX platforms. MMND has a pipe mode so it can be run with an X-Windows or other windowing system wrapper. Hunger has generously placed the source code in the public domain. MMND as released on 10/8/96 is available on the CUG CD-ROM as volume #459.

Support Resources

e-mail: a.hunger@hulmecc.nwnet.co.uk

CUG 460   Yet Another Class Library: Multiplatform Framework

M.A. Sridhar of the University of South Carolina (Columbia, SC) contributes Yet Another Class Library (YACL), an innovative cross-platform application framework. YACL is a C++ class library that offers high-level abstractions for common programming problems. Its design goal both is to be application-centric and to take advantage of C++ facilities (e.g., operator overloading and templates) wherever possible. YACL implements both scalar (String, Integer, Date, etc.) and container (sequence, set, tree, etc.) core classes. The GUI classes are based on a variation of the model view controller (MVC) paradigm. YACL supports all expected GUI objects (menus, dialogs, buttons, listboxes, button groups, etc.) and resources (cursors, fonts, pens, colors, and brushes).

The YACL application framework supports the widest variety of compilers, GUIs and OSs I've ever seen in a freeware library, including Windows 3.1, Windows NT, OS/2 2.x and 3.0, SGI, SUN, Ultrix,

Linux, RS/6000, and HP-UX. YACL v1.60 as released on 11/11/96 is available on the CUG CD-ROM as volume #460.

Support Resources

e-mail: sridhar@usceast.cs.sc.edu
WWW: http://www.cs.sc.edu/~sridhar/yacl.html

CUG 461   Railroad Signaling Modeler

Dean Lance Smith and Mohammad Musa present their paper "Two Software Data Organizations that Support Railroad Signaling" and accompanying C source. This program models a control system capable of understanding an entire railroad line composed of any combination of automatic blocking system (ABS) and centralized traffic control (CTC) blocks. In railroad parlance, a "signal block" or "block" is a length of rail track that is controlled by a block signal. A block may contain two or more tracks in various track configurations. Most blocks have at least one main track. Two or more main tracks may also be in parallel in a block. A block may also contain lines that cross the main track(s), turnouts, branch lines, or sidings. Two or more blocks constitute a rail line.

The package contains both the signal modeler data entry program and a second program capable of combining several adjacent blocks into single blocks. The programs are designed for MS-DOS using Borland C but could probably be ported to other environments by modifying the display code (which uses INT 10h). Railroad Signaling modeler as released on 1/3/93 is available on the CUG CD-ROM as volume #461.

Support Resources

e-mail: dsmith@scs.howard.edu

CUG 462   Sherlock v2.0 for Macintosh: Debugging Tools

Ed Ream (Madison, WI) submits the Sherlock v2.0 set of debugging tools for Macintosh as CUG volume 462. Earlier incarnations appeared as Sherlock v1.7 for MS-DOS (CUG 355) and Macintosh (CUG 356). Sherlock is a debugging tool different from currently popular interactive debugging tools such as CodeView. Sherlock uses C macro expansion capabilities to implant debugging calls and functions without manual coding. Those calls are enabled/disabled from the command-line, and removing those calls from the source is also done automatically. Sherlock uses far less memory than a full-size debugger. In addition, Sherlock provides detailed statistics about your program.

The volume contains full source code for all portions of Sherlock, along with all test files, batch files, executable files, and detailed documentation. Sherlock is in the public domain and may be used for any commercial or non-commercial purpose. Sherlock can be used in Motorol MC68xxx or PowerPC Macs. Sherlock v2.0 as released on 4/8/96 is available on the CUG CD-ROM.

Support Resources

e-mail: `edream@mailbag.com`

CUG 463   LInteger: Arbitrary Precision Integer Class Library

Leonard Janke (University of British Columbia, Vancouver) contributes LInteger, a C++ library that empowers you to create and perform arithmetic on objects representing nearly arbitrary precision integers. Thanks to C++ support for operator overloading, the use of the large integers in this library should be nearly as easy as the use of regular `int` types. In many cases, converting your application to use LInteger can be as simple as substituting `LInteger` for `int` in your editor.

The current version of this library requires Intel 386 or better CPU and is guaranteed to compile perfectly only with GNU C++. LInteger originally appeared on the Linux platform and has now been ported to Windows NT. Janke predicts it should work with OS/2 or Windows 95 with only "minor hacking." He has coded the multiprecision methods in assembly language for speed. Multiplication can be performed via recursion or Montgomery style. It also supplies implementations of FIPS hashing algorithm and pseudo-random number generation. LInteger includes documentation in HTML for public methods. This library is free for both commercial and non-commercial use. LInteger v0.2 as released on 9/2/96 is available on the CUG CD-ROM as volume #463.

Support Resources

e-mail: `janke@unixg.ubc.ca`
WWW: `http://www.interchg.ubc.ca/janke/linteger`
FTP: `ftp://ftp.funet.fi/pub/crypt/math/`

CUG 464   Miracle C Compiler for MS-DOS

B.T. Szocik (Ottawa, Ontario) submits the Miracle C compiler, a complete language and run-time implementation for MS-DOS. Szocik intends Miracle C to be used primarily as a teaching support tool. Miracle C supports only the small memory model (code < 64Kb, data < 64Kb). Pointers are always 16-bits; no "far" extensions are allowed. All K&R C syntax and data types are fully supported (plus some ANSI extensions) — there's nothing small about the language implementation.

Miracle C generates .obj object code files but does not include a linker. You may be able use the LINK.EXE supplied with some versions of MS-DOS or use one provided on the Microsoft software library site (such as ftp://ftp.microsoft.com/softlib/MSLFILES/lnk563.exe). Miracle C does include a 45-page users manual and run-time library reference in Word for Windows and ASCII formats.

Since Miracle C is distributed as shareware, you must register it if you plan to use it beyond the evaluation period. Registration is only U.S. $15, and entitles you to full compiler source code of the next version. Miracle C compiler v1.6 as released on 10/3/96 is available on the CUG CD-ROM as volume #464.

Support Resources

e-mail: bg283@freenet.carleton.ca
WWW: http://www.ncf.carleton.ca/~bg283/

CUG 465   Fader Custom Control for Windows

Victor R. Volkman (Ann Arbor, MI) contributes his Fader custom control for Windows, a slider control for use with Windows 3.1 and compatible environments. The fader is a custom control designed to return a continuous range of values based on the position of a thumb that slides along a rail. This idea is similar to the Windows scrollbar in many respects. Since the scrollbar is almost inseparably associated with scrolling the client area, it quickly becomes unfamiliar in other contexts. The fader provides an analog range in the same way the potentiometers are used in a stereo equalizer or mixer. For example, a fader could be used to apply equalization to a waveform or to regulate the hue of a color.

Fader compiles under Microsoft C/C++ or later. The archive includes an accompanying 10-page tutorial on custom controls, which originally appeared in *Windows Developers Journal*, Feb/Mar 1992.

Fader is in the public domain and may be used for any commercial or non-commercial purpose. Fader as released on 2/1/92 is available on the CUG CD-ROM as volume #465.

Support Resources

e-mail: sysop@HAL9K.com
WWW: http://www.HAL9K.com

CUG 466   Autoduck: Automated API Documentation Extraction

Eric Artzt of Microsoft Corporation (Bellevue, WA) releases Autoduck, a Windows 95/Windows NT console utility that extracts specially tagged comment blocks from C/C++, Visual Basic, and Assembly source files. Autoduck formats the information in the comment blocks and produces documentation files in Rich Text Format (RTF) for use with Microsoft Word or the Windows Help Compiler. Autoduck can also produce HTML files for Internet or intranet use.

Autoduck is an extremely easy and efficient way to produce nicely formatted documentation files for your programming interfaces. The program extracts information from tagged comment blocks and from the language elements themselves. The tagset supports most C/C++ constructs, including classes, member functions, function, enumeration types, structures, etc. Autoduck includes full source code in C++ and requires MFC. Autoduck v2.00.96.1220, as released on 12/20/96, is available on the CUG CD-ROM as volume #466.

Support Resources

e-mail: ericartzt@accessone.com
WWW: http://www.accessone.com/~ericartzt
FTP: ftp://ftp.accessone.com/pub/ericartzt/

CUG 467   LADsoft 32-Bit ANSI C Compiler for 386 and M68k Families

David Lindauer (Louisville, KY) submits his LADsoft C compiler, an optimizing cross-compiler that can produce either Intel i386 or Motorola M68000 assembly language output. To produce DOS-mode code, you'll need an assembler such as Borland TASM and TLINK linker. The compiler contains optimizations and also has separate code generation switches for M68000, M68010, and M68020 CPUs. The compiler recognizes some C++ syntax as well, except for class declarations. LADsoft C strives to be ANSI compatible at the source level. It may fall short of requirements for evaluation ordering when casts are used. Also floating point is done purely using the math coprocessor, and is not adjusted for ANSI/IEEE compatability. The run-time library is designed to be ANSI compatible. The CUG volume includes full source for compiler and library as well as compiled executables. LADSoft C v1.35, as released on 3/5/97, is available on the CUG CD-ROM as volume #467.

Support Resources

e-mail: `gclind01@starbase.spd.louisville.edu`
FTP: `ftp://ftp.std.com/pub/os-code`

CUG 468 Programmable Arbitrary Precision Calculator for Windows

S. Jason Olasky (Rockville, MD) submits his Programmable Arbitrary Precision Calculator for Windows (PAPCW). PAPCW is a reverse polish notation (RPN) line-oriented calculator for Windows 3.1, Windows 95, and NT. It includes financial and date functions in addition to many standard mathematical functions. The extended precision math routines utilize Judson D. McClendon's `Bigcalc` extended precision library. Virtual arrays are used for the stack and memory registers, so there are no effective limits on the stack size or number of registers. The stack is based on the FORTH model rather than the HP calculator model; the stack expands and contracts as numbers are entered or result from operations on numbers already on the stack. PAPCW programs use a hybrid notation combining elements of the HP-41 and FORTH. Programs can be written using any ASCII Editor or through a rudimentary built-in editor. Calculator dialogs facilitate use of the financial and date functions. A registration fee of $35 is required for use beyond the evaluation period. The CUG volume includes full C source code. PAPCW v1.1, as released on 12/7/96, is available on the CUG CD-ROM as volume #468.

Support Resources

e-mail: `70471.2501@compuserve.com`

CUG 469   V: A Platform-Independent GUI Library for C++

Bruce E. Wampler (University of New Mexico, Albuquerque) releases V, a portable C++ GUI framework intended to support a wide variety of applications on different graphical interface platforms. Applications developed using V will have the look and feel of the native platform, yet will be portable across platforms. Most standard GUI objects are supported by V, including windows with menus, status bars, tool bars, and a drawing canvas; modal and modeless dialogs with the most common controls, and portable printing support. V was originally written for use on XWindows and has since been ported to Windows 3.1 and Win32 environments. The XWindows implementation has been validated on Linux, SunOS, and Alpha, and SGI machines. In MS Windows, it has been built succesfully with Borland, Watcom, and Microsoft VC++. OS/2 and Motif ports are underway and should be completed soon. V is licensed under the GNU Public License, which is intended to preserve its freeware status. The CUG volume includes separate archives for XWindows and MS Windows. v1.16 of V, as released on 1/20/97, is available on the CUG CD-ROM as volume #469.

Support Resources

e-mail: wampler@cs.unm.edu
WWW: http://www.cs.unm.edu/~wampler
FTP: ftp://ftp.cs.unm.edu/pub/wampler

CUG 470   src2www/fm: Hypertext Index for Program Listings

Michal Young (Purdue University, Hammond, IN) contributes a pair of packages for producing program listings with hypertext indexes. These packages do not automatically indent code; a code-formatting utility (such as GNU indent, CUG volume #392)) or pretty-printing text editor should be used prior to using src2www or src2fm. src2www produces HTML versions of ANSI C and Ada code as well as simple C++ code. Building the binaries requires GNU make, Flex, and GCC from the Free Software Foundation. Also, a recent version of gawk or nawk will be needed by the scripts. src2fm shares the same front end, and therefore processes the same languages, but produces FrameMaker documents. FrameMaker document colors and fonts can be customized using style sheets, while customizing the HTML documents requires editing a table compiled into the program. src2www and src2fm have been implemented only on UNIX systems. Young is willing to provide advice to those attempting a port to non-UNIX platforms. According to Young, "a good C programmer should be able to add a driver for another output format, such as RTF or LaTeX." src2www and src2fm are distributed as freeware. src2www v0.9g and src2fm v0.9e are available on the CUG CD-ROM as volume #470.

Support Resources

e-mail: `young@cs.purdue.edu`
WWW: `http://www.cs.purdue.edu/people/young`
FTP: `ftp://ftp.cs.purdue.edu/pub/young`

CUG 471   Beagle: Client/Server DBMS for UNIX

Robert Klein (Glen Burnie, MD) submits Beagle, an SQL-based client/server relational DBMS. Currently, Beagle supports a wide variety of UNIX platforms, including: Linux 2.0.14, SCO Openserver, FreeBSD 2.1R, SGI IRIX v5.3, Solaris v2.x, and HP/UX. The current version also supports OS/2, and porting projects are underway for Windows 95, NT, and other platforms. A support mailing list is available too. Beagle's features are accessible primarily through its C-callable API. Its client/server implementation works using BSD style sockets for communication. Most of the recent development has centered around implementing BTree indexes and seeing that they are properly applied in SELECT, DELETE, and other SQL statements. Beagle DBMS, as released on 4/3/97, is available on the CUG CD-ROM as volume #471.

Support Resources

e-mail: `robk@pulse-sys.com`
WWW: `http://tiny.iapnet.com/rob/beagle.html`
FTP: `ftp://www.iapnet.com/pub/beagle`

CUG 472   HELIOS: Radiosity (Photorealistic) Renderer for Windows

Ian Ashdown (West Vancouver, BC) releases HELIOS, a radiosity renderer for Windows. "Radiosity" is the name used by the computer graphics community to describe radiative flux transfer techniques. Radiosity methods are extremely useful in developing advanced lighting simulation and visualization software for architectural design and illumination engineering applications (see the following figure). Radiosity is in a sense the complement of ray tracing. Ray-tracing techniques excel in the rendition of point light sources, specular reflections, and refraction effects. Radiosity methods accurately model area light sources, diffuse reflections, color-bleeding effects, and realistic shadows. Ashdown wrote HELIOS as an integral part of his book *Radiosity: A Programmer's Perspective*, (ISBN 0-471-30488-3), John Wiley & Sons, New York, 1994. The HELIOS source code is copyrighted, but freely available for personal, non-commerical uses. The CUG volume of HELIOS includes complete C++ source code and executables for a fully functional radiosity renderer that runs under MS-Windows 3.1, Windows 95, and Windows NT. HELIOS v1.03, as released 4/1/96, is available on the CUG CD-ROM as volume #472.

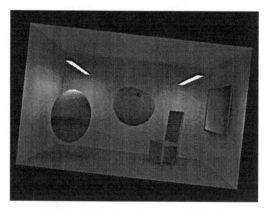

A sample image rendered by HELIOS

Support Resources

e-mail: iashdown@ledalite.com
WWW: http://www.ledalite.com
FTP: ftp://ftp.ledalite.com

CUG 473   HotKey: Windows 95-Style Taskbar for Windows 3.1

Hao Liang (Zongshan, People's Republic of China) contributes HotKey, a Windows 95-style taskbar for Windows 3.1. HotKey can be used by itself or it can coexist with PCTools for Windows desktop (by Central Point Software). In addition to organizing tasks and their icons, HotKey includes a pop-up zoom window (F12 key toggles),

RGB value display (F11 key), and absolute position display wherever the mouse cursor roams. HotKey is written using Borland C++ 4.5. Rather than using MFC or OWL, Liang has created his own lightweight GUI framework. HotKey also includes a copy of John Webster Small's popular container_lite, a portable container library for C++. The CUG Library volume of HotKey includes full C++ source and executables. HotKey, as released on 1/17/97, is available on the CUG CD-ROM as volume #473.

Support Resources

e-mail: zhboai@pub.zhuhai.gd.cn

CUG 474   The X Games

Matt Chapman (Bournemouth, England) submits a trio of games for the X Windows environment: XScrabble, XCountdown, and XBikes. XScrabble was co-written with Matthew Badham. The programs also incorporate Xc, the Control Panel Widget Set v1.3 by Paul D. Johnston. Chapman has granted permission for these programs to be freely copied and distributed by any means, provided that his copyright notices remain unchanged. He reserves the right to be identified as the author of the programs.

Support Resources

e-mail: matt@belgarath.demo.co.uk
　　　　mchapman@hursley.ibm.com
WWW: http://www.belgarath.demon.co.uk/programs

CUG 474A   X Games: Multiplayer Scrabble with 114K Words

XScrabble is a full multiplayer (1–4) implementation of the classic board game (see the following figure), with multilevel computer players, and over 118,000 word dictionary (the Official Scrabble Players Dictionary, edition 3, as used in U.S. tournaments). There is a high-score table, a best-single-goes list, a handy setup window, and load/save facilities. XScrabble should work in most X-Window environments, including SunOS 5.1, AIX, and Linux. The CUG Library volume includes full source code in C. XScrabble v1.00, as released on 3/12/97, is available on the CUG CD-ROM as volume #474A.

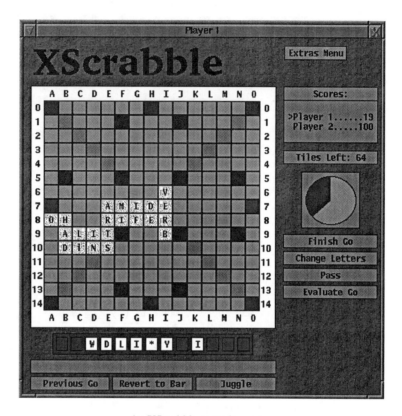

An XScrabble game in progress

CUG 474B   X Games: Countdown UK Quiz Show Game

Countdown is a daily British quiz show involving word games and number games. XCountdown is a two-player implementation of the show, for the X Window System. Each player has their own game window on their own display. The included OSPD (Official Scrabble Players Dictionary, version 2 — all words up to 9 letters) is used for the word games. Various algorithms are used to show the best possible score for each game, after the players have attempted it. XCountdown also contains some pictures of Carol Vorderman, who is featured on the show. XCountdown should work in most XWindows environments, including SunOS 5.1, AIX, and Linux. The CUG Library volume includes full source code in C. XCountdown v1.00, as released on 2/12/97, is available on the CUG CD-ROM as volume #474B.

CUG 474C   **X Games: Lightcycle Game for Two-to-Six Players Over Net**

XBikes is a very simple light cycles games for two to six players. The "light cycles" game idea was first popularized by the movie *Tron*. BSD sockets are used for client/server communication so each player can play from their own X console. Each player controls their "bike," which keeps moving until it hits something, while leaving a trail behind it. Your path must not intersect another player's path, your own path, or the walls of the playing field. The sooner you crash, the more points you lose. The last player still moving is declared the winner. XBikes requires an XWindows environment, only Solaris is currently supported. The CUG Library volume includes full source code in C. XBikes v1.00, as released on 2/12/97, is available on the CUG CD-ROM as volume #474C.

CUG 475   ThinAir: Pseudo-Random Number Generator in C++

G. Wade Johnson (Houston, TX) contributes ThinAir, a C++ class library providing an abstract interface to pseudo-random number sequence generator (PRNG) classes. The library is distributed as source and documentation for over 40 PRNGs, including algorithms by Knuth, Borosh-Niederreiter, Waterman, RandGen, and Marsaglia. ThinAir is designed to take the guesswork out of using PRNGs. Unfortunately, most PRNGs available to the average programmer are not very good. Usually it's not easy to learn which generator is provided. This makes finding the weaknesses or problems with a particular generator almost impossible. Even if you realize the potential problems with a provided generator, you usually don't know how to go about testing and verifying another PRNG. ThinAir allows you to take control of which PRNG you want in order to get the quality and integrity you need. The CUG Library volume includes makefiles for VC++, Borland C++, and GNU C++. ThinAir features a rand() interface, function object interface, the ability to save and restore state on a generator, and the ability to clone a generator. ThinAir is released as freeware, and though Johnson retains copyright to the source, there are no restrictions on using it in your applications. ThinkAir v0.9B, as released on 2/20/97, is available on the CUG CD-ROM as volume #475.

Support Resources

e-mail: gwadej@anomaly.org
WWW: http://www.anomaly.org

CUG 476   Amulet: Portable C++ GUI Application Framework

Brad A. Myers of the User Interface Software Group in the Human Computer Interaction Institute at Carnegie Mellon University submits Amulet. Amulet is a user interface development environment for C++ and is portable across X11 on all kinds of UNIX (Sun, Dec, HP, SGI, Linux, NetBSD, etc.), Microsoft Windows 95 and NT (with VC++), and the Macintosh. Amulet helps you create graphical, interactive user interfaces for your software. More than just another free virtual toolkit, Amulet includes many features specifically designed to make the creation of highly-interactive, graphical, direct-manipulation user interfaces significantly easier, including a prototype-instance object model; constraints; high-level input handling with automatic undo, built-in support for animation, and gesture-recognition, and a full set of widgets. Amulet is the successor to Garnet, an earlier CMU project you may have known. Amulet v3.0 is available on the CUG CD-ROM as volume #476.

Support Resources

e-mail: bam@cs.cmu.edu
WWW: http://www.cs.cmu.edu/~amulet

CUG 477   Using C++ and FORTRAN: Tutorial on Mixed Languages

Carsten Arnholm (Heggedal, Norway) contributes his paper "Portable Mixed-Language Programming Using C++ and FORTRAN" and accompanying class libraries. This treatise considers how best to encapsulate calling FORTRAN libraries from the C++ environment in both MS Windows and UNIX platforms. Arnholm notes that 40 years of legacy FORTRAN code and its maintenance should and must continue to be used in many cases. He sets forth rigorous guidelines for mixed-language integration:

- The C++/FORTRAN programs must be as portable as their FORTRAN-only ancestors.
- A single source code must be used on all platforms.
- Calling FORTRAN from C++ must be easy and straightforward. It must not be significantly more difficult to call FORTRAN from C++, than from FORTRAN itself.

- Mixed C++/FORTRAN must not induce any significant performance penalty.
- All major FORTRAN features must be supported from C++.
- Calling FORTRAN from C++ shall be done without changing the FORTRAN code, which has been tested and verified.

Arnholm's package consists of the 30-page paper (.wri file), FORTRAN.H macros, and CHARACTER, COMPLEX, and FMATRIX compatability classes. Draft Revision 5, as released on 3/16/96, is available on the CUG CD-ROM as volume #477.

Support Resources

e-mail: ca@dnv.com

CUG 478   FreeDOS: 16-bit MS-DOS Replacement with Sources

Morgan Toal (Barrow, AK) releases FreeDOS, a completely free MS-DOS compatible operating system. FreeDOS will run on all DOS capable platforms, from XTs to Pentium Pros. FreeDOS is a complete standalone operating system. It includes a kernel, shell (COMMAND.COM replacement, and a full complement of utilities (from ATTRIB to XCOPY). FreeDOS is using a freeware C compiler for all development work. The FreeDOS mission is to allow hobbyists, hackers, and anyone who would enjoy a chance to examine or customize the source code and inner workings of a real operating system for educational, practical, or recreational purposes. FreeDOS is be compatible with MS-DOS v3.30. FreeDOS and its associated programs and documentation are protected under the terms of the GNU General Public License (GPL). All copyrights are retained by the original authors. All source code will be publically available. FreeDOS v0.92.0, as released 2/7/97, is available on the CUG CD-ROM as volume #478.

Support Resources

e-mail: mtoal@arctic.nsbsd.k12.ak.us
WWW: http://sunsite.unc.edu/pub/micro/pc-stuff/freedos/
         http://www.freedos.org

CUG Volumes 300–399

CUG 300   MAT_LIB: Matrix Library

MAT_LIB (Matrix Library) is a shareware package submitted by John J. Huges III (TN). MAT_LIB includes approximately 50 C functions and macros that input and output tabular data maintained in ASCII text files. Although the tabular data is in RAM, it is stored in dynamically allocated token arrays or floating-point arrays on the heap. Functions that examine an ASCII text file to determine the number of rows, columns, and token size of the tabular data in the file are provided. Other C macros dimension either a floating-point or string token array large enough to hold the ASCII data. Once in memory, floating-point array matrix operations can be performed on the data. Token array data can be converted to and from float or integer values. Floating-point arrays that have been modified by calculation can be merged into a token array for output or they can be output to a text file directly. The output files can in turn be used as the input for later application programs found in MAT_LIB text file formats. The volume includes a users manual, test programs, example programs, and small and medium model libraries for Turbo C.

CUG 301   BGI Applications

This volume contains graphics applications that use Borland Graphics Interfaces (BGI). All programs were compiled with Turbo C and use BGI files. This volume includes C source code, executable code, and BGI files. Mark A. Johnson (CO) has created DCUWCU, a simple application environment that provides a mouse-driven cursor, stacked pop-up menus, and forms that contain editable fields and a variety of selectable buttons. The sample program DRAW allows you to draw lines, circles, and text on the screen using a mouse. A stacked pop-up menu can be invoked anywhere on the screen. DRAW uses public domain Microsoft mouse routines written by Andrew Markley.

Henry M. Pollock (MA) has submitted a demonstration program combining trig functions and graphics functions in Turbo C. By selecting an option from the menu, the program displays circleoids, asteroids, spirals, cycloids, etc.

John Muczynski (MI) has created a graphics pull-down menu system with deeply nested menus. The included code allows you to change key assignments and create macros. The new configuration may be saved and restored. He also has submitted an example program, *Conway's Game of Life*, using the pull-down menu.

CUG 302   3-D Transforms

Written by Gus O'Donnell (CA) and submitted by Michael Yokoyama (HI), 3-D Transforms is a library of functions used to create, manipulate, and display objects in three dimensions. The functions allow the programmer to create representations of solid objects bound by polygons, to rotate, translate, scale the objects in three dimensions, and display the objects in color with a given light source. The volume includes a brief description of each function in the library, complete C source code, function libraries for Turbo C, and a demonstration program that displays a cube, a tetrahedron, and an octahedron in three dimensions with each figure rotated about a different axis. The program requires a Turbo C graphics library and BGI files. Turbo C v1.5 or later is recommended.

CUG 303   MC68K Disassembler

Written by John M. Collins (England), MC68K Disassembler runs on Motolora 68000 ports of UNIX System III and V. The disassembled output can be assembled to generate the same object module as the input. When disassembling stripped executable files, object modules and libraries may be scanned, modules in the main input identified, and the appropriate names automatically inserted into the output. Also, an option is available to convert most non-global names into local symbols, reducing the number of symbols in the generated assembler file. The disassembler copes reasonably with modules merged with the -r option to ld, generating a warning message as to the number of modules involved. The volume includes a users guide and complete C source code. Although the program is MC6800-specific, it is easily adaptable to run in most any operating system environment as a cross-development tool. The COFF object file can now be taken as input and disassembled.

CUG 304   ROFF5: Technical Text Formatter

Ernest E. Bergmann (PA) has completed a major rewrite of his ROFF4 (CUG 128 and CUG 145). The ROFF5, v2.00, technical text formatter has evolved from ROFF4 to become somewhat more like UNIX's nroff and troff. ROFF5 now supports conditional macros, page traps, roman numerals, and line numbering. It is intended for preparation of manuscripts on any dot-matrix printer and can handle equations and special symbols. Different output devices are supported with device-specific ASCII files that inform ROFF5 of the special controls for that device. Fractional line spacing for superscripts and subscripts are supported even for printers that cannot reverse scroll. The built-in commands follow the naming conventions of nroff and troff where appropriate; however, in contrast to the UNIX formatters, ROFF5 supports register and macro names of arbitrary length. The volume includes a complete set of C source code, well-written documentation, and a number of test and demo files. The program was written using Turbo C v2.0 for MS-DOS.

CUG 305   Hercules Graphics Adapter

CUG 305A   HGA Mandelbrot Explorer

Dan Schechter has submitted a Hercules monochrome Mandelbrot program, as well as the card games poker and blackjack. Unlike most Mandelbrot programs, which require you to specify color-value information in advance, his programs EMANDEL and EJULIA save all calculation data, allowing you to tweak the picture by specifying color-value information afterwards.

CUG 305B   HGA BlackJack and Draw Poker

POKER is five-card-draw poker. The computer plays four hands independently (the computer's four players do not consult with each other) and you play one hand. BLACKJACK is not-quite-real casino blackjack. It is just you against the dealer. Doubling down is not supported. The screen display of both card games is neatly organized using the Hercules graphics. This volume includes C source codes as well as executables for MS-DOS. All the programs are compiled using the Aztec C compiler.

CUG 306   Thread and Synapsys

CUG 306A   Thread: Multitasking Kernel with Lightweight Threads

Gregory Colvin (CO) has contributed Thread and Synapsys. Thread is a multitasking kernel based on lightweight threads. He uses the ANSI Standard C library functions, `setjmp()` and `longjmp()`, to implement multiple threads within a single C program. He has tested the code with Microsoft C v5.0 on an IBM-AT, and with MPW C v3.0 on an Macintosh SE. On his AT machine, the kernel compiles to under 1Kb of code and executes over 80,000 jumps per second.

CUG 306B   Synapsys: Neural Network Simulator

Synapsys is a neural network simulation program that implements a very fast back-propagation network by representing synapse layers as word arrays and implementing all operations with integer arithmetic. The volume includes C source code, benchmark, and testing code for both programs.

CUG 307   ADU and COMX

CUG 307A   ADU: Alien Disk Utility

ADU, submitted by Alex Cameron (Australia), is a disk utility program designed to work with both the IBM PC standard and non-PC disk formats. By choosing an option from the main menu, ADU can analyze the disk format, then read and write the contents of the disk, sector by sector. The menu is also user-configurable so that the disk parameters can be adapted to almost any conceivable disk format. The initial alien disk parameters are derived by scanning the disk and building up a `disk_base` table, which may then be modified by the user. The volume includes C source code and well-written documentation revealing the low-level detail of the PC's disk drive configuration, not available anywhere else. The program is compiled under Turbo C v2.0 or v1.5. No assembly is required.

CUG 307B   COMX: Serial Port Driver for MS-DOS

COMX, an MS-DOS communication port device driver submitted by Hugh Daschbach (CA), provides buffered I/O to a serial port with optional XON/XOFF flow control through standard read/write requests or interrupt 0x14. The program uses mixed memory models. COMX.C is compiled under the small model with explicitly declared far pointers, and a front-end program forces the linkage editor to produce a tiny model executable. This program is specifically written for Microsoft C (v5.0 or later) and some assembly code comes with the C source code.

CUG 308   MSU, REMZ, and LIST

CUG 308A   MSU: Simulates a Hypothetical Computer

Dinghuei Ho (WA) has submitted MSU, an educational simulation of simple computer architecture and operation. MSU can simulate a computer that has a 4Kb word memory space (each word is 32 bits), a CPU that includes four segment origin registers; instruction register, program status register, a card reader and line printer for input/output, and a clock. The program runs under VMS on the DEC VAX 8820, but you can port it to other environments by modifying the code.

CUG 308B   REMZ: Parks-McClellan-Remez FIR Filter Design

Bob Briggs (CA) has submitted REMZ, the classic Parks-McClellan-Remez FIR filter design program based on the FORTRAN version appearing in *Theory and Application of Digital Signal Processing* by L.R. Rabiner & B. Gold (Prentice Hall, Englewood, N.J., 1975. ISBN 0139141014). The program compiles under Turbo C or Quick C.

CUG 308C   LIST: Object-Oriented Linked List in C and C++

Michael Kelly (MA) has submitted LIST, an object-oriented implementation of a linked list using both C and C++. In C, LIST is able to imitate C++ notation (address_list.sort()) by defining a general structure whose fields are pointers to functions, each corresponding to the operations of an object. Version 2.01 of LIST allows an unlimited number of active lists.

CUG 309   6809 C Compiler for MS-DOS

Brian Brown (New Zealand) has ported CUG #221 6809 C for FLEX to MS-DOS. Modifications allow the program to run with ASxxxx assembler (CUG #292), as well as with Motorola AS9 assembler. The program also generates ROMmable code. The volume includes a complete set of C source code, well-written documentation, and a run-time library such as routines for controlling the ACIA serial port, functions for character handling and data conversion between character strings and integers, routines for controlling a Hercules card, routines for a magnetic card reader, memory manipulation routines, PC serial card functions, and string-handling functions.

CUG 310   Little Smalltalk for MS-DOS

This Little Smalltalk, submitted by Henri de Feraudy (France) is part of Smalltalk Express Ltd.'s (England) effort to bring the object-oriented paradigm to the general public. They ported Timothy Budd's Little Smalltalk to three different, low-cost platforms: the IBM-PC, the Atari ST, and a British machine called the Acorn Archimedes. This particular volume is for MS-DOS. The volume includes the source code and executable files, but no documentation. You can learn more about Smalltalk in *A Little Smalltalk*, by Timothy Budd, published by Addison-Wesley (1987), ISBN 0201106981. The program was compiled under Microsoft C v4.0. The original UNIX version of Little Smalltalk is also available from our library (CUG #229 and CUG #230).

CUG 311   Relational Database with ISAM

Ken Harris (WI) has contributed his database routines, DB package v1.3. The DB package consists of a library of file-handling routines that may be linked with user applications. The routines support the following file organizations: sequential (data records of fixed length are stored sequentially), index (data records are stored in an ISAM type organization), random (data records of variable length are stored sequentially). The routines include basic database manipulation routines such as addition, deletion, and search, and also sort routines. The DB package lets you develop a data object dictionary to create a relation between two data records. The volume includes all C source code and test files, and a users guide that describes each routine. The program has been compiled and tested under Ultrix on a VAX station-2000 with gcc, using Microsoft C v5.1 and Turbo C v2.0 under MS-DOS, and cc under UNIX on 3B1.

CUG 312   Make-Maker: AWK-Based Analyzer Builds Makefiles

Contributed by Jim R. Yehle (CO), Make-Maker automates the process of creating a makefile. Make-Maker is a series of AWK programs that first scans C source code for #include files to build a dependency list (a makefile component, called a Dependency Generator), then scans a linker configuration file to build a primary target dependency list (object file extractor), and finally builds a full makefile. Since the linker configuration file is unique to each linker, you must create your own object file extractor. The volume includes object file extractors for the Turbo Link Response file and the Intel Linker (binder) configuration file. The volume also includes Intel 80x86 assembly and PL/M dependency generators, as well as a C dependency generator. All the AWK code takes advantage of the 1985 enhancements to the original 1977 AWK.

CUG 313   STEVIE: Multiplatform Vi Text Editor

The STEVIE editor by Tony Andrews (Boulder, CO) is a highly portable clone of the popular UNIX "vi" editor. STEVIE first appeared on the Atari ST platform and its name stands for "ST Editor for VI Enthusiasts." However, the current version of STEVIE can be compiled for the Atari ST running TOS or Minix, UNIX System V or BSD, and PCs running MS-DOS or OS/2. Others have reported success in porting STEVIE to the Amiga and Data General machines, although platform-specific code for them is not included in this release. In any case, the CUG volume does not include any binary executables so you must compile it yourself before you can run it.

STEVIE displays text with ANSI terminal emulation escape sequences. These escape sequences were popularized by the DEC VT-100 series of terminals. Ideally, ANSI terminal support provides maximum display portability with minimum programming effort. For PCs, you'll need an ANSI accelerator such as NANSI.SYS by Daniel Kegel (Altadena, CA). STEVIE does not check for the presence of ANSI emulation and will render an illegible set of escape strings if it is missing.

Because STEVIE v3.71 was released in 1989, the documentation claims compatability with only Microsoft C 5.1 in the MS-DOS environment. However, I compiled the STEVIE source code without errors using the Microsoft C 6.00A. The quality of the source code could be improved with the addition of ANSI function prototypes.

CUG 314   MNP: Microcom Networking Protocol

Written by Gregory Pearson (CA), Microcom MNP C Library is a set of subroutines that implements the stream model (Class 2) of the Microcom Networking Protocol (MNP) link protocol. MNP link protocol's stream mode works with MNP error-correcting modems or with other software implementations that use the Microcom MNP Library or other compatible software. The program is suitable for use with a Microsoft C application using the small code/small data model. The volume includes C and assembly source code for the library, a programmer's guide, and a sample terminal emulation program.

CUG 315   FTGRAPH: Fast-Fourier Transform Plus Graphics

Contributed by Thomas R. Clune (MA), FTGRAPH is a set of utilities for performing Fourier transforms and inverse Fourier transforms. The program also performs operations such as multiplication of data files, auto-power spectrum, cross-power spectrum, correlation from power-spectrum data, and filter time-domain real data. The result can be displayed on the monitor or printer, or saved as an HPGL file. The program will use a math coprocessor (8087, 80287, or 80387) if present, but does not require it. The program supports Hercules, CGA, EGA, and VGA graphics cards. A Microsoft (or compatible) mouse can select an option from the menu. The volume includes a complete set of C source code including a mouse driver, documentation, and sample data files such as a 16-cycles square wave, a Gaussian waveform, a sine and cosine wave, and a noisy Gaussian curve. The program is copyrighted by the Eye Research Institute.

CUG 316   AS8: Cross-Assembler for Zilog Z8

Contributed by H. G. Willers, this volume includes a cross-assembler for Z8 microprocessor. The assembler is based on the code of a cross assembler for a Z80 processor from DECUS and enhanced with a hashed symbol table and several bug fixes. The source code compiles under MS-DOS using Mark Williams' Let's C (v3.0.3) and QuickC (v1.01) and under System 5.3 UNIX for 68020 and Interactive UNIX for 386. The volume includes C source code, a users guide, and test files.

CUG 317   Group 3/4 Image Processing (TIFF)

Michael P. Marking (AZ) has submitted a set of programs that manipulate facsimile or scanner graphics images. These programs include techniques to encode and decode Group 3 (or 4) images and techniques to extract and insert TIFF (Tag Image File Format) image files in C. The C source code should be fairly portable, though it was developed with Microsoft C v5.1 under MS-DOS.

CUG 318   RED: Compact Text Editor Handles Big Files

Edward K. Ream (WI) has placed his commercial software, the RED text editor, in the public domain. RED v7.0 is a full-screen text editor written as an exercise in information-hiding techniques. RED provides an edit mode, an insert mode, an overtype mode, and searching that allows wild cards, replacement, undo, and block operations. RED achieves two technical accomplishments without sacrificing portability: the screen is updated quickly, and arbitrarily large files are handled quickly. The size of the .exe file is very small, only 35Kb. RED compiles with Microsoft C v5.0 or later and Turbo C v2.0 under MS-DOS. Make and link files have been included for both compilers. The source code has been revised to take advantage of the latest features of the draft ANSI standard of January, 1988. Function prototypes and other modern features are used throughout. The volume includes complete C source code, excellent documentation, make files, and programs with a debugging session of Ed Ream's Sherlock debugging system (CUG #355 for MS-DOS or CUG #462 for Mac).

CUG 319   CPP: Industrial-Strength ANSI C Pre-Processor

Edward K. Ream has placed his commercial software CPP (C preprocessor) in the public domain. CPP v5.3 is a modern C preprocessor that conforms to the ANSI C standard, but will complain about duplicate macro definitions. CPP provides several command-line options to include comments in the output file, define an identifier, allow nested comments, specify search paths for #include files, and cancel the effect of the first definition of a macro. CPP will compile with Microsoft C v5.0 or later and Turbo C v2.0 under MS-DOS. Both compilers include make and link files. The source code uses the features of the draft ANSI standard of January 1988. The volume includes complete C source code, excellent documentation, make files, and programs with a debugging session of Ed Ream's Sherlock debugging system (CUG #355 for MS-DOS or CUG #462 for Mac).

CUG 320   Convolution Image Process

This volume, contributed by Wesley G. Faler (MI), contains a program that implements an image manipulation algorithm called convolution. The program takes an image file as input, applies the convolution algorithm to the image, and generates a new image. Supports only the CUT ("Dr. Halo") input file format. The program was developed under MS-DOS using Turbo C v2.0 and its Borland Graphics Interface (BGI) features. The volume includes C source code, documentation, and sample scanned image files.

CUG 321   Mouse Trap Library

This shareware package, written by James M. Curran (NJ), contains a collection of functions to control a mouse. These functions provide easy access to the low-level functions of the mouse interrupt, as well as a simplified system for defining buttons or hot spots on the screen. The volume includes Small and Large model libraries for Microsoft C v5.1, a sample test program, and documentation that describes each mouse function.

CUG 322   Doctor's Tools

This volume contains four programs: Trace by William M. Rogers (NJ), RAM Test by Dean Lance Smith, Mkptypes by Eric R. Smith (Canada), and Malloc Leak Trace by Michael Schwartz (WA). The volume includes all the C source code and documentation for each program.

CUG 322A   Trace: Macros for Debugging

Trace is a collection of debugging macros. Using ANSI C features such as __FILE__ and __LINE__, these macros provide enough information to trace the execution of a program.

CUG 322B   RAM Test: ATS Tests for Defective Chips

RAM Test, written by Dean Lance Smith with Mohammad Khurrum and Chaiyos Ruengsakulrach, is an implementation of the ATS (Algorithmic Testing Sequence) algorithm developed by Knaizuk and Hartman and the ATS+ algorithm developed by Nair. The program tests RAM for any single or multiple stuck-at-0 or stuck-at-1 faults. These programs can be compiled under MS-DOS using Turbo C.

CUG 322C   Mkptypes: Generates ANSI C Prototypes

Mkptypes is an ANSI prototype generator that takes one or more C source code files, and produces a list of function prototypes for the external functions defined in the input source files. The program is written in Standard C.

CUG 322D   Malloc Leak Trace: Tracks Lost Memory

The Malloc Leak Trace package is designed to help trace dynamic memory allocation leaks. The package provides the standard `malloc`/`free`/`realloc` interface, but keeps track of all `malloc`'d buffers, including their size, order of call, and address.

CUG 323   Explod and Beyond the Tesseract

CUG 323A   Explod: Fireworks Graphics Display

Explod was contributed by Dennis Lo and David Lo (Canada). A graphics program, Explod generates an animated fireworks display. Explod works with Hercules, VGA, EGA, or CGA graphics cards. By specifying options on the command line, you can control some performance parameters such as video type, the number of simultaneous explosions on the screen, delay factor, the number of explosions to display before exiting, and the effect of gravity and wind. The volume includes a complete set of C source code and assembly files, sample explosion data files, executable code, and documentation. Explod compiles with Turbo C v1.5 or later and requires MASM v5.0, but can be compiled with other compilers by changing the segment and group names.

CUG 323B   Beyond the Tesseract: A Text-Based Adventure Game

David Lo has written an adventure game called *Beyond the Tesseract*. This adventure game recognizes two-word verb-noun commands for moving, taking inventory, manipulating objects, and saving the game. The program recognizes about 200 words. The volume includes C source code and documentation. The program compiles under Turbo C v1.5 or later.

CUG 324 WGCONIO: TSR-Compatible Text Windowing

WGCONIO Library, contributed by William Giel (CT), is a set of text-windowing functions that emulate most of Turbo C's text-windowing functions. Giel created the library after discovering that some of Turbo C functions didn't work when the application program was memory resident. The library provides box drawing, cursor manipulation, keyboard control, window manipulation, shadowing, and text editing in windows. The volume includes C source code, documentation, a sample program and small-model library. Although the library was developed using Turbo C v2.0, it should be compilable using other C compilers by replacing int86() calls with the corresponding routines of your compiler.

CUG 325 Zia VGA Graphics Library

This shareware VGA graphics library contributed by Ismail Zia (U.A.E.) contains routines for filling a region with specified pattern and color, setting up a view port, drawing an area bigger than the physical screen, saving and loading a screen image; drawing a rectangle, ellipse, polygon, line, and arc with specified line style and color; and transforming, scaling, and rotating an object, etc. The program works on VGA standard modes and some extended modes. The volume includes a huge model library for Microsoft C v5.0 or later and a large model library for Zortech C/C++ v2.0, documentation that describes all the functions in the library, demo animation image files, programs, and batch files, font files, and executable stroked font editor. Since the program was developed in C and 80386 Assembly (not included in the volume), it will run under MS-DOS only on a 386 machine.

CUG 326 SoftC Database Library: Access dBASE III/III+/IV Files

This shareware package, submitted by Jan Schumann (SoftC Ltd., MN), provides 120 functions for fully compatible access to dBASE III/III+ and dBASE IV data, memo, and index files; and Clipper and Foxbase index files. The volume includes complete documentation, header file, demo programs, and small memory model libraries for Turbo, Zortech, and Microsoft C. Version 2.1 provided new features: the support for dBXL, Quicksilver data and FoxPro memo files, functions added to perform record I/O with users' structures, and object code libraries for Zortech C++, Turbo C/C++, and Microsoft Quick/

Professional C. Version 3.0 provides full dBase IV support, fully automatic record and file locking, faster re-index functions, user-extensible Index Expression Evaluator, faster index searches, and more compact index files. Windows DLL support is available from the vendor.

CUG 327   Panels for C: Text Windows and Menus

J. Brown (KS) contributed Panels for C, a shareware package containing user interface routines (windows and menus) for the IBM PC. Unlike other window libraries, screen fields and attributes that are defined in an ASCII text file are interpreted at run-time. Thus, fine-tuning user interfaces is possible without recompiling the program. The volume includes a small model object code for Microsoft C, and demo C source and executable code. The current version (v2.3) provides Turbo C support, adds an Interactive Panel Design (IPD) utility, and allows the inclusion of panel definitions in C source programs by utilizing the PATH environment variables to find panel definition files.

CUG 328   WTWG: Windows Text / Windows Graphics

WTWG v1.2 is a public-domain software package with routines for Windows Text mode or Windows Graphics mode, submitted by David Blum (CA). It provides drawing boxes, overlapping windows, mouse-selectable buttons, scroll bars, save/restore screens, text/graphics mode operations, pull-down and pop-up menus, context-sensitive help, programmer-definable hot keys, keyboard macros, transparent integration of mouse and keyboard, and a virtual memory system using expanded memory, RAM, or disk space. The volume includes all the C source code that can be compiled under Turbo C v2.0/C++ or Microsoft v5.1; demo C source and project/batch files; utilities for online help, keyboard macros, and file manipulation; and documentation.

CUG 329   UNIX Tools for PC: Classic Text Manipulation Tools

This volume contains a collection of submissions. Most of the programs were derived from some UNIX commands and rewritten to compile under MS-DOS or OS/2. The volume includes all the C source code.

- Robert Artigas, Jr. (TN) has ported UNIX utilities, cat (concatenate files), cut (cut out selected fields of each line of a file), tr (transliterate characters), wc (word count), vis (visual display of files) and egrep (regular expression matcher search utility) to MS-DOS and OS/2 environments. egrep uses regular expression functions developed by Henry Spencer (Canada).

- Martin D. Winnich (CA) has modified a cross-referencer, XC, using Microsoft QuickC. The program is now called XCXREF and processes more symbols from input text.
- Arkin Asaf (Israel) has contributed cflow, define, and dprintf. cflow is a program that displays a function dependency tree from input C source files. The program doesn't preprocess and parse the code, but it does a good job of displaying the function dependency tree. It distinguishes between function definition and function declarations.
- Henry de Feraudy (France) has submitted a string substitution utility, csubst. csubst extracts strings or substitutes strings in C source code. The string extraction helps create a substitution. makefiles for Turbo C, Mark Williams C, Zortech C, and QuickC are included as well as the C source files.

CUG 330   CTask: Priority-Based Preemptive Multitasker

CTask v2.2, contributed by Thomas Wagner (West Germany), is a set of routines that allows a C program to execute functions in parallel, without a programmer building in sophisticated polling and switching schemes. CTask handles the switching of processor time with a priority-based, pre-emptive scheduler to provide routines for inter task communication, event signaling, and task interlocking. The package includes drivers for MS-DOS serial I/O, printer buffering, and concurrent access to DOS functions. To compile CTask, Microsoft C v5.1 or later, or Turbo C v2.0 or later are required. Microsoft MASM v5.1 or later, or TASM v1.01 or later is required for the assembly parts. The volume includes well-written documentation, C and assembly source code, library modules for Microsoft C and Turbo C, make files, and sample application source code.

CUG 331   SE Editor: Text Editor with A Stack

Contributed by Gary Osborn (CA), SE is a revision of the GED editor (CUG #199), which is a revision of the e editor (CUG #133). This version uses up to 500Kb of RAM for text storage, while functioning with as little as 6Kb of allocatable memory. A stale page directory has doubled the virtual disk system's efficiency. An embedded runoff function will reformat internal text as per dot commands, and a text push stack has been added for pushing and popping lines. The undo capability has been extended to include redo. The program supports free cursor movement. The command and display structure has been enhanced, but still retains WordStar compatibility where feasible. The program was developed under Microsoft C v4.0. The volume includes C source code, documentation, and an executable file.

CUG 332   PCcurses: UNIX Terminal-Independent I/O

Written by Bjorn Larsson (Sweden), this volume includes the PC-curses v1.4 cursor/window control package. PCcurses offers the functionality of UNIX curses, plus some extras. Normally, you should be able to port curses-based programs from UNIX curses to PCcurses without making changes. PCcurses is a port and rewrite of Pavel Curtis's public domain ncurses package. All the code has been rewritten. The volume includes C and assembly source code, user documentation, makefiles for various compilers, and a public domain make executable file. In addition, the volume includes some game programs such as stone, bugs, jotto, yahtzee. This program can be compiled under Microsoft C v3.0, 4.0, 5.1, or Turbo C v1.0, 2.0 or 68K Paragon C. MASM is required for the assembly file.

CUG 333   gAWK: GNU AWK for DOS and OS/2

Bob Withers (TX) has modified the GNU version of AWK. This gAWK version provides all the features and functionality of the current UNIX AWK version, except for using pipes and user-defined functions. The program was developed under Microsoft C v5.1 and can be executed under MS-DOS and OS/2. The volume includes C source code, Yacc source, makefile, user documentation, sample AWK programs, and AWK executable file. Yacc (CUG #285 Bison) is required to compile the Yacc source.

CUG 334   GNUPLOT: Plots Mathematical Functions or Data

Written by Thomas Williams and Colin Kelley; modified by Russell Lang, Dave Kotz, John Campbell; and submitted by Henri de Feraudy (France), GNUPLOT v2.02 is a command-driven interactive function plotting program with bit mapped graphics routines. By typing commands interactively or loading a text file that contains commands, users can draw graphs or plot data points on screen in a given graphics mode or on a printer using a given printer driver. GNUPLOT provides a set of commands: loading/saving command file; plotting a function (built in or user-defined) or data files; printing a title, label, or arrow on a graph; clipping data points; specifying graphics mode (CGA, EGA, VGA if PC), line style, grid, ranges, offset, scaling size, sampling rate, polar/rectangular coordinates; turning on/off auto-axis scaling or auto-tic marks; output redirection; online help; and escaping to shell. Built in mathematical functions are the same as the corresponding function in the UNIX math library, except that all functions accept integer, real, and complex arguments. The sgn function is also supported as in BASIC.

GNUPLOT supports the following graphics and printer drivers: AED 512, AED 767, BBN BitGraph, Roland DXY800A, EEPIC, Epson LX-800, Fig, HP2623, HP2648, HP75xx, HPGL, IBM Proprinter, Imagen, Iris4D, Kermit-MS, LaTeX, NEX CP6 pinwriter, PostScript, QMS QUIC, ReGis (VT125 and VT2xx), Selanar, Tek 401x, Vectrix 384, and UNIXplot. For the PC version, it supports IBM CGA, EGA, MCGA, VGA, Hercules, AT&T 6300, and Corona 325 graphics. Version 2 has added parametric functions, X11 Motif support, and printer drivers for Epson 60dpi printer, Tandy DMP-130 printer, Star color printer, emTeX, AT&T 6300, Tektronix 410x, X11, HP LaserJet II, VT like Tektronix emulator, Kyocera Laser printer and SCO CGI. The volume includes a complete set of C source files for the program and graphics driver; makefile for UNIX, Microsoft C, and Turbo C; documentation; and demo command files. The program has compiled under UNIX, VMS, and MSDOS (using Microsoft C or Turbo C).

CUG 335   Frankenstein Cross-Assemblers: Many 8- and 16-Bit CPUs

Written in a combination of Yacc and C, Frankenstein includes a series of cross-assemblers for 8- and 16-bit microcomputers: RCA 1802–1805, Signetics/Phillips 2650, Hitachi 6301–6303, 64180, Mos Technology/Rockwell 6502, Motorola 6805, 6809, 68hc11-6801–6800, Texas Instruments tms7000, Intel 8041–8048, 8051, 8085, 8096, Zilog Z8, and Z80. The programs were developed and tested under UNIX/XENIX and MS-DOS systems. Turbo C v1.5 was used for MS-DOS. Yacc or Bison (CUG #285) is required to build executable code.

CUG 336 EGAPAL/EDIPAL: EGA Graphics and Palette Editors

This volume includes EGA graphics applications and utilities contributed by Scott Young (NH) and Marwan El-Augi (France). Young's shareware package, EGAPAL, is a series of programs allowing users to create EGA graphics images for the 640x350 and 16-color mode. EGAPAL includes a graphics image editor program, a utility that converts the graphics image into a header file to be included in your C programs, and a library that loads a graphics image from disk or header files to the screen. The package requires Turbo C and includes documentation and a sample program. El-Augi's palette editor, EDIPAL, allows the user to change the EGA palette and save it. Saving the new palette is implemented by not closing the graphics system — therefore the change is not permanent.

CUG 337 Designing Screen Interfaces in C

This volume contains the source code that appeared in James Pinson's book *Designing Screen Interfaces in C* (paperback 267 pp., published by Yourdon, February 1991, ISBN 0132015838, distributed by Prentice Hall). The volume includes C source code for screen/window functions such as pop-up menus, moving light bar menus, and multilevel moving light bar menus. The code will compile under all memory models of Turbo C and Quick C.

CUG 338 68000 C Compiler and Assembler for MS-DOS

The cross-development tools for MS-DOS from Brian Brown (New Zealand) include a 68000 C compiler, which was adapted from CUG #204 68K C compiler and assembler, adapted from CUG #261 68K cross assembler. The compiler uses both intermediate and peephole optimization and generates very efficient 68000 assembly code. It accepts floating-point types but doesn't know how to deal with them. The preprocessor supports only #include, and #define. There is no standard run-time library support. The volume includes the C source code and MS-DOS executable code for both compiler and assembler and documentation. The source code will compile under Turbo C. Currently, no commercial use of the programs is allowed.

CUG 339   CTRLCLIB: Manage Ctrl-C, Ctrl-Break, Reboot

This shareware package from William Letendre (NJ) is a collection of C functions to help programmers manage user-inititated interrupts such as Ctrl-C, Ctrl-Break, lock keys, and reboot sequences. Properly handling these interrupts is one of the hardest things an MS-DOS developer will run up against. The volume includes small and large memory model libraries for Microsoft C v5.1 and v6.0, Quick C v2.5, Turbo C v2.0, and Turbo C++ v1.0, and sample demo programs.

CUG 340   C-Window: Interactive Screen Format Generator

This shareware package from Josef Ebnet (Germany) is an interactive screen-format generator, C-Window 3.0. C-Window provides a user-interface editor that creates windows, pop-up/pull-down menus, and variable-length data entry fields with user-specified attributes. The output C source code is compiled under Microsoft/Quick C, Turbo C, or Lattice C. The volume includes the form editor, sample programs, and small model object modules for Microsoft/Quick C, Turbo C, and Lattice C.

CUG 341   Orbit Propagation: Solves Kepler's Two-Body System

Includes several orbital mechanics utilities submitted by Rodney Long (MD). A two-body, Keplerian orbit propagator that uses the universal variables method; a solver for Kepler's equation; a conversion routine for converting between true and eccentric anomaly; a conversion routine for Keplerian to Cartesian coordinates; a conversion routine for Cartesian to Keplerian elements; plus period, semi-latus rectum, true, and eccentric anomalies are all provided for educational purposes. The volume includes all the source code, MS-DOS executable code, input test data, and the resulting output data. The program was developed and compiled using Microsoft C v5.1.

CUG 342   I8255 Interface Library: Drive CBI/Metrabyte Board

Submitted by Blake Miller (AL), this library includes a collection of routines for digital I/O using a Computer Boards Inc. CIOAD-16, or a Metrabyte PIO12 compatible digital I/O board containing at least one Intel 8255 Programmable Peripheral Interface integrated circuit. The functions include initialization of data space, configuration, clear/read/

write the bytes in the 8255, etc. He has also provided a more general and advanced digital I/O library. The volume includes all the source code for the library, small/medium/large model library, make files, and test/demo programs.

CUG 343　C Image Processing System: Filtering and More

Dwayne Phillips (VA) has provided the source code and TIFF (Tag Image File Format) files for the C image processing system (CIPS). CIPS is a small system that combines image processing operators with a simple user interface. The source code is compiled using Microsoft C v6.0. Although certain display manipulation calls are unique to Microsoft, the substitution of these calls with equivalents from other C compilers, such as Turbo C, is possible.

C Image Processing System's main calling routine provides a user interface for performing various image-processing operations, such as filtering, rotations, scaling, cutting, pasting, and rotating. Also provides image addition/subtraction, half-tone display, edge detection, and histogram equalization.

CUG 344　C Grab-Bag #1: Strings, Data Structures, Math, etc.

A collection of small C utilities contributed by 11 authors. Most of the programs were developed under MS-DOS, but some programs are portable enough to be compiled under other operating systems. The volume includes complete C source code for all programs.

- Eric Horner (IL) has submitted XTAB (tab extraction utility), ITAB (tab insertion utility), PCON (multiple printer control codes), and MIND (mastermind game). The programs are portable, although they were developed under Turbo C v2.0.
- Michael Kelly (MA) has submitted functions for parsing a line of text into an array of strings, substring search in a string, and low-level primitives for quick screen output in text modes on IBM PC or compatible. He has also provided the demonstration programs using those functions and Turbo Pascal source code indent utility. The programs were developed under Turbo C v1.5/2.0.
- Paul Ammann (CT) has submitted a pull-down menu demonstration program that was developed under Turbo C and uses a BGI file. The current setting works for CGA terminals.

- Ronald J. Terry (IL) has submitted various mathematical functions (exp, ln), which use fast converging series approximations, IBM video functions, DOS functions, and string functions. The programs were developed under Turbo C.

- Bryan R. Leipper (NV) has submitted a printer utility that prints input files to a printer with HP LJ II+ graphics. The program provides an extensive set of options to set margins, height of page, tab expansion, width of line, output direction, pages to print, the number of copies, page header and footer, and nonprintable characters as underlined byte values. The program was compiled under Microsoft C v5.1.

- Vernon R. Martin (OH) has submitted a set of functions similar to BASIC functions, used when a C program must access a BASIC data file or a BASIC program needs to be ported into C. The BASIC-like functions are: instr() [in string] function; mid(), right(), cvd() and ncvs(), which unpack packed double or single precision data into a double value; and mkd() and mks(), that pack a double value into an eight-or four-character long string. The programs were developed under XENIX C compiler or ECO C compiler.

- Adam Blum (VA) has contributed P2S, which converts printf() in C programs to C++ streams formatted I/O (<< operator). It handles width and precision flags (%-6.2f) by generating the appropriate streams manipulators — setw() and setprecision(). The source code is a lex source file; thus you need Flex (CUG #290) to compile the program.

- Bill Forseth (MN) has contributed MTX, which solves a matrix Alb form using Gauss-Jordan elimination. This program uses dynamic allocation of memory and executes quickly. This program was developed under Turbo C v2.0.

- Michael Wiedmann (Germany) has contributed a set of functions to access the resident portion of PRINT.COM in MS-DOS. Using those functions in an application program, a user can print from the application, stop printing, and resuming printing. The program was developed under Microsoft C v5.1/ 6.0.

- D.N. Holland (PA) rewrote CFLOW, which prints a C function tree based on input C source code. The new CFLOW provides features such as adding line numbers, wild cards, f flag that is used to find the first level functions only. He also provided the versions of CB and XC2 programs in CUG #236.

- Conrad Thornton (LA) has submitted a set of functions to manipulate a circular queue. Any size and any data type can be stored in the queue. Those functions can be used for event trapping.

CUG 345   The Last Cross-Referencer: Reads C or Pascal Progs

Contributed by Edouard Schwan (CA), TLC/TLP is "The Last C-Cross Referencer and The Last Pascal-Cross Referencer." The referencer reads one or more source files and generates a source file listing (with line numbers) and a cross-reference list for the non-reserved symbols in the file(s). The referencer provides several command-line options to support debugging and indirect command line specification. Developed under Aztec C65 v3.2b, AppleIIGS APW C v1.0, and Apple Macintosh MPW C v3.0. However, they should be easily ported to an MS-DOS environment. The volume includes C source code and some documentation.

CUG 346   ASxxxx Cross-Assembler Part 2: 68HC16 CPU

Alan R. Baldwin has added another cross-assembler to his ASxxxx Cross-Assemblers (CUG #292). Because of CUG 292's size, we have created a new volume for this assembler. The new cross-assembler is for the 68HC16 16-bit microprocesser. The assembler has been tested using DECUS C under TSX+ and RT-11, PDOS C v5.4b, and Turbo C v1.5 under MS-DOS. The volume includes C source code for the assembler, executable code for the assembler and linker, documentation, and testing assembler files.

CUG 347   TAVL Tree: Threaded AVL Optimizes Traversal Time

Contributed by Bert C. Hughes (MN), TAVL Tree (v2.0) is an implementation of a hybrid data structure, the threaded height-balanced tree. The height-balanced tree, or AVL (Adelson-Velskii-Landis), tree corrects the performance degradation on a traditional binary tree by re-balancing the tree as necessary whenever items are inserted or deleted. However, with traditional binary or AVL trees, it is not efficient to move from any given node to its successor or predecessor. To find the successor of a given node in a binary or AVL tree, you must walk through the entire tree in order until you arrive at the node whose successor you wish to find. The next-in-order node is the desired successor. Finding the predecessor is done similarly.

Threaded binary trees solve this problem by replacing the nil links in leaf and half-leaf nodes with links to the node's in-order successor (or predecessor or both). Threads are distinguished from links with an additional two-bit field in each node: one bit for each child link. With this additional information, the procedure for moving to a successor node becomes simple and does not require a stack or recursion. The volume includes C source code for TAVL tree routines, sample make-files, example programs using TAVL routines, and documentation. The programs are written in Standard C.

CUG 348   8048 Disasembler and 280 Assembler

Contributed by Michael G. Panas (CA), this volume includes two public domain programs: 8048 disassembler and Z80 assembler.

CUG 348A   8048 Disassembler

8048 disassembler generates an output file that contains Intel 8048 mnemonics from an 8048 binary input file. The output file can be reassembled by any Intel-type assembler for 8048, such as a48 from Will Colley (CUG #219). The disassembler was developed under Microsoft C v5.1 on MS-DOS, and UNIX V Release 3.2. Z80 cross-assembler was developed based on Will Colly's a48 assembler.

CUG 348B   Simple Z-80 Assembler

The assembler assembles the dialect of Z-80 source code into Z-80 object code. All assembler features are supported except relocation, linkage and macros. The assembler was developed and tested under Microsoft C v5.1 on MS-DOS, and Altos System V UNIX and Xenix 3.0. The volume includes documentation, C source code, and executable code for UNIX and MS-DOS.

CUG 349   Simulation Subroutine Set: Discrete Event System

Contributed by M. A. Pollatschek (Israel), the shareware package Simulation Subroutine Set (SSS) is a library that makes writing a discrete event system simulation program in any high-level language (C, Pascal, Basic, FORTRAN) as easy as using a dedicated simulation language such as GPSS, Simula, SIMSCRIPT, SIMAN, etc. Discrete event system simulation imitates interacting processes developing in time, usually involving random phenomena on a digital computer. Typical applications include maintenance scheduling, inventory policy, distribution design, staffing, planning, advertising, analysis of operations, etc. The volume includes an installation batch file, manual for library routines, tutorial for simulation using SSS library, and SSS libraries for Microsoft's Quick Basic, Quick C, Quick Pascal, FORTRAN, Turbo C, and Pascal. Due to the volume and MS-DOS specific nature of the program, libraries and manuals are archived by PKXARC.

CUG 350   PCX Graphics Library: Read and Display Files w/VGA

Ian Ashdown (Canada) has submitted a PCX Graphics Library, PCX_LIB (v1.00C). PCX_LIB is a library of functions for displaying and storing Zsoft's Paintbrush® PCX-format image files. It was developed expressly for release into the public domain. Fully commented ANSI C source code is provided for all functions, along with complete technical specifications for ZSoft's PCX image file format. The current version supports the display and storage of images on MS-DOS equipped with Hercules, CGA, EGA, MCGA, or VGA. SuperVGA and XGA display adapter are not supported in this release. The volume contains documentation including PCX image file format specifications, PCX_LIB source code, demonstration programs, sample PCX image files, and a batch file to build the library under Microsoft v6.0.

CUG 351   UltraWin: Fast Text Windows for MS-DOS

The UltraWin shareware package, contributed by Kevin Hack (MO), is a small and fast text windowing library that allows unlimited windows. It was written specifically for systems that use text displays with many windows that overlap and update real-time in the background. An extensive array of output functions is available, with full-color control, scrolling (both up and down), and masking capabilities. Input functions are included for data entry such as strings, dates, prices, and even user-definable templates. The volume includes documentation, demo programs, and a small model library for Turbo C v2.00 or Turbo C++ v1.0. The current version, v2.10, includes new features: unlimited overlapping windows, background printing, PC timer control, mouse and graphic support, enhanced data entry capabilities, a hypertext help engine, and EGA/VGA font editor. A supplement program, InTuition (v1.10), is a textual user-interface library that includes an interface construction program that allows using a mouse interactively to create dialog boxes, menus, pick lists, and forms.

CUG 352   String and Vlist Class Libraries

CUG 352A   String Class Library: Uses Operator Overloading

David Blum (CA) has contributed a collection of routines written in C++. A class, String, provides BASIC-like string processing such as Substring, Replace, Find (an enhanced version of strstr(), strchr(), strcspan(), and strpbrk()), and Tokensize. The class also provides the ability to write statements such as:

```
String A, B, C;
if (A==B)   ...// compares string
                // contents, not pointer addresses
A = B + C;   // concatenate strings
```

CUG 352B   Vlist Class Library: Dynamic Lists of Pointers

A class, Vlist, provides a flexible array of pointers to data objects, and allows creation of dynamic lists of pointers designed to work with String as well as Blum's earlier Window Text mode or Window Graphics mode (WTWG CUG 328). Supplementary routines include filename and directory handling, a simple ASCII file editor (using WTWG), and some pop-up menu routines. The volume includes C++ source code and header files. The programs were developed under Turbo C++.

CUG 353   C++ Tutor: A Self-Paced Course

Gordon Dodrill, Coronado Enterprises (NM), has submitted his shareware package, C++ Tutor v2.0. C++ Tutor is a comprehensive instructional course for the C++ programming language. The volume includes 12 chapters of text (about 115 pages), a number of example C++ programs, and some exercises with answers. The tutorial text covers topics such as pointers, functions, encapsulation, inheritance, multiple inheritance, virtual functions, etc. The accompanying example programs are meant to be studied, compiled, and run while you read the printout of the tutorial text. This tutorial will assume a thorough knowledge of the C programming language. The descriptions and instructions are applicable to Borland's implementation of C++. The C version of this tutorial, C Tutor, is also available from us as CUG #252 and CUG #253.

CUG 354 CES Mouse Tools Library: Includes Joystick Support

John F. Jarrett has contributed a shareware version of Computer Engineering Service Mouse Tools Library with JoyStick Functions (v 1.25). The library has over 50 functions that deal only with Microsoft-compatible mice. These functions give you almost complete control over mouse motion and sensing in all of your programs. In addition, the library also includes joystick functions that are hardly seen in C. The joystick functions work with most all joystick game controllers that use the standard addresses starting from 200H. The functions sense button presses and X and Y movement on two joysticks allowed by most game adapters, including some needing a Y cable. The volume contains header files; documentation; and the medium memory model compiled for Turbo C v2.0, Turbo C++, Borland C++, QuickC v1.0, Microsoft C v6.0, and Mix Power C v2.0. There is also a QuickBasic #include file for using the C functions with QuickBasic and a couple of demostration executables and source.

CUG 355 Sherlock for MS-DOS: Automatic Debug Code Insertion

Edward K. Ream (WI) has placed all of the Sherlock v1.7 debugging package into the public domain and contributed it all to the CUG Library. Sherlock was formerly a commercial product and represents more than four years of programming effort.

Sherlock is a debugging tool different from traditional interactive debuggers. Sherlock uses C macro expansion capabilities to implant debugging calls and functions without manual coding. Those calls are enabled/disabled from the command line and removing those calls from the source is also done automatically. Sherlock offers great advantages over interactive debuggers, especially when it comes to the development of memory-hogging applications, because Sherlock's overhead is small. In addition, Sherlock provides detailed statistics about your program.

The volume contains full source code for all portions of Sherlock, along with all test files, batch files, executable files, and detailed documentation. For the MS-DOS version (CUG #355), the code was developed and tested using Microsoft C v5.0 and Turbo C v2.0. Make files and link files are provided for both compilers. For the Macintosh version (CUG #462), the code was developed using Think C v2.0 and then ported to MPW. Sherlock has been tested with System 7 and System 6 with MultiFinder. The Macintosh version of Sherlock differs in several important respects from the MS-DOS version: the Sherlock Preprocessor has been extensively revised and uses an object-oriented library. Due to the subdirectories included in the volume, the format is restricted to MS-DOS (CUG #355) or Macintosh (CUG #462).

Support Resources

e-mail: edream@mailbag.com

CUG 356   Sherlock for Macintosh

Reissued as CUG volume #462.

CUG 357   CSTAR: Hybrid C/ASM 68000 Cross-Compiler

Edward K. Ream has also placed all of CSTAR into the public domain. The CSTAR language is essentially a superset of K&R C with some extensions to allow assembly code to be specified in a C-language format. The CSTAR compiler is a cross-compiler: it runs on MS-DOS and produces Digital Research (CRI) format 68000 assembly language output. It would be simple to change the output to another 68000 format, but changing to another target machine would be difficult. CSTAR produces locally optimal code in almost all circumstances: it produces code for arithmetic operations and flow of control constructs that is at least as good as would typically be produced by an expert assembly language programmer. The CSTAR language extensions include the ability to treat C variables that have the same name as 68000 registers as if they were register variables assigned to the corresponding register; the ability to treat functions that have the same name as 68000 instructions as if the corresponding 68000 instruction were inserted in line; and finally, the #enum preprocessor directive, an abbreviation for a sequence of #defines.

CSTAR doesn't support ANSI C features such as blocks (all variables of a function must be declared as formal parameters), bit fields, complex initializers involving arrays of structs or unions, enum data type, or function prototyping.

By combining the front end of SPP tool (Sherlock Preprocessor in CUG #355 and #462) with the back end of the CSTAR compiler, one could create a full ANSI C compiler, although it wouldn't be very easy.

The volume contains full source code for all portions of CSTAR, along with all test files, batch files, executable files, and documentation. The source code for CSTAR can be compiled using Miscrosoft C v5.1 or later, or Turbo C v1.5 or later. make files and link files for both compilers are provided.

Support Resources

e-mail: edream@mailbag.com

CUG 358   cbase: Multiuser B+Tree ISAM DB File Library

Lyle Frost (IN) has contributed a shareware version of cbase programs. cbase is a complete multiuser C database file management library, providing indexed and sequential access on multiple keys. It features a layered architecture and comprises four individual libraries:

- cbase — C database library for indexed and sequential access
- lseq — doubly linked sequential file management library
- btree — B+-tree file management library
- blkio — block buffered input/output library

cbase internally uses lseq for record storage and btree for inverted file index storage, which in turn uses blkio for file access and buffering. blkio is analogous to stdio but based on a file model more appropriate for structured files such as those used in database software. The lower-level libraries can also be accessed directly for use independent of cbase. For example, the btree library can be used to manipulate B+-trees for purposes other than inverted files, and the blkio library can be used to develop new structured file management libraries. cbase is written in strict adherence to ANSI C standard while it maintains K&R C compatibility. All operating system dependent code is isolated to a small portion of the blkio library to make porting to new systems easy. Currently, UNIX and DOS systems are supported. For UNIX systems, the programs were tested under Interactive UNIX; for DOS systems, Turbo C (v2.0), Turbo C++, and Microsoft C v5.1 were used for compiling. The volume includes documentation, complete source code for cbase (v1.0.2), and a sample rolodeck card program.

CUG 359   GNU C/C++ for 386: 32-Bit Compiler and Library Source

Written by Free Software Foundation, ported to DOS by D. J. Delorie, and submitted by Henri de Feraudi (France) and Mike Linderman (Canada), this package contains a 32-bit 80386 DOS extender with symbolic debugger, a C/C++ compiler with utilities, development libraries, and source code. It generates full 32-bit programs and supports full virtual memory with paging to disk. The package requires a 80386-based IBM compatible PC or PS/2. The 80387 emulator currently does not emulate trancendental functions (exp, sin, etc.). Approximately 4 to 5 Mb of hard drive space is required. 640Kb RAM is required. The following hardware is supported:

- up to 128Mb of extended (not expanded) memory;
- up to 128Mb of disk space used for swapping;
- SuperVGA 256 color mode up to 1024x768;
- 80387;
- XMS & VDISK memory allocation strategies; and
- V86 programs such as QEMM, 386MAX, DesqView, Windows/ 386 are not supported.

The volume includes binary executable files: C/C++ compilers, LALR(1) parser (Bison), lexical parser (Flex), C/C++ preprocessor, 80386/80387 assembler, a.out (BSD) format linker (ld), archive utility, symbol stripper, compilation coodinator, basic 32-bit DOS extender, symbolic debugger, etc. In addition, libraries that support standard routines, math routines, graphics, and mouse routines (compiled with gcc, source code included), #include-header files, documentation, sources for extender and various VGA/SuperVGA drivers, diffs from FSF distributions to DOS-compatible, sources for the utilities, sample C++ sources using graphics and mouse, and 80387 emulator for non-80386 systems. Due to the volume of files and DOS nature of programs, all files are archived by PKZIP (unzip utility is also included) and the archived file is separated into pieces by split utility. Thus, we restrict the volume format to MS-DOS. Source code for the C compiler is not included.

Support Resources

WWW: http://www.delorie.com

CUG 360   USpell: Spell Checker Optimized for UNIX

Bill McCullough (MO) has contributed a spell checker program, Uspell. Uspell is basically a modification of CUG #217 Spell, optimized to improve the performance under UNIX systems. The optimization techniques Uspell uses include: replacing scanf with a single read, retaining the whole index in memory, converting input words to

5-bit format before spell checking, reading the dictionary in increments of file system blocks caching locally, eliminating stdio functions, etc. The volume includes C source code for spell checker, ASCII text dictionary, compressed dictionary and index files, and a utility used to compress the ASCII text dictionary.

CUG 361   Gadgets and Term

CUG 361A   Gadgets: UNIX-Like Tools for MS-DOS

Jack E. Ekwall has contributed a function library Gadgets, a group of UNIX-like tools for DOS. Gadgets provides functions such as pop-up/drop-down window, drawing box, screen and cursor manipulation, keyboard input, color, date, printer and mouse control, and file manipulation. Some of the functions are lifted from CUG #273 Turbo C Utilities. The library is linkable to Turbo C v2.0. These UNIX-like tools offer a solution to the DOS command-line interface pipeline problem.

CUG 361B   Term: A Computer Buzz-Word Glossary

Jack E. Ekwall has also contributed Term, a collection of computer buzz-words. Term includes 634 topics and 32 historical notes/observations about computer buzz-words. This text is in a text-indexed sequential form that can be read by a display program, VU. The volume includes source code for the library and documentation.

CUG 362   RMAXTask: Priority-Based Cooperative Multitasking

Contributed by Russ Cooper (AZ), RMAXTask (a shareware version) is a library of C functions that lets you run one or more C functions together in a priority-based, cooperative, multitasking environment in which a task continues running until it explicitly relinquishes control by making a call to the multitasking system. RMAXTask provides full support for intertask synchronization and communication, timed delays, and access to the PC's keyboard.

RMAXTask provides a more capable scheduler and better intertask communication than do simple round-robin task switchers such as Wayne Conrad's MTASK, while avoiding the complexity of a full-blown, interrupt-driven, preemptive system such as Thomas Wagner's CTask (CUG #330).

The volume includes a large model of the library, complete documentation, a demo program, and short test programs. To obtain the source code for the library, you may contact Russ Cooper at RMAX Development Group, 1033 East Coral Gables Drive, Phoenix, AZ 85022.

CUG 363   68020 Cross-Assembler for MS-DOS

This 68020 Cross-Assembler v1.0 is an upgrade of the 68000 assembler written by Paul McKee of North Carolina State University in 1986, and released to the public domain by Marwan Shaban. Andrew E. Romer (England) has added the 68020-specific mnemonics (excluding the math-coprocessor mnemonics), and introduced minor modifications. The source code has been modified to conform to the ANSI C Standard and can be compiled under Microsoft C or Zortech C v3.0 compilers.

The volume includes the complete C source code, makefile, documentation, assembler executable, and assembly source files for testing.

CUG 364   C-Across: Cross-Reference Multiple C Modules

C-Across, by Myron Turner (Canada), is a cross-reference utility for multiple module C programs. The v1.02 update includes minor bug fixes. The program produces six indexes of functions, prototypes, and globals that enable a user to see across modules for use in checking and comparison. Function names are listed in hierarchical form, showing the relationship between caller and callee for functions. Globals are listed in schematic descriptors that record all modifiers and qualifiers and enable checking of declarators across modules. C-Across optionally generates a header file that includes prototypes from function definitions. It is also possible to list user-defined types and some preprocessor #defines. The volume contains a complete set of C source code, DOS executable code, and full documentation. The program was developed and tested under Microsoft QuickC.

CUG 365   Elvis: vi and ex Clone Text Editor

Contributed by Steve Kirkendall (OR), Elvis (v1.5) is a clone of vi/ex, the standard UNIX text editor. Elvis supports nearly all of the vi/ex commands, in both visual mode and colon mode. Like vi/ex, Elvis stores most of the text in a temporary file instead of RAM. This allows it to edit files that are too large to fit in the data space of a single process. Also, the edit buffer can survive a power failure or crash. Elvis runs under BSD UNIX, AT&T SysV UNIX, SCO XENIX, Minix, MS-DOS (Turbo C or MSC v5.1), Atari DOS, OS9/68000, Coherent, VMS, and AmigaDOS. The volume includes a manual for Elvis (over 70 pages), a complete set of source code for the supporting operating systems, `makefiles`, and TROFF format documentation files. In addition, it comes with source code for utilities that preserve and recover a text buffer after a crash, generate `tags` file from C source, display a C function header using `tags`, and adjust line length for paragraphs of text.

CUG 366 MicroEMACS: Portable and Extensible Text Editor

MicroEMACS CUG #366 updates a popular, portable, extensible CUG editor to a new version (3.11) and to new volumes in the CUG Library (formerly CUG #197 and #198, v3.9). The new version includes a new help system, a new windowing system supporting mulitple screens and mouse manipulation, portable file locking, support for more machines and systems, better handling of line terminators on input and output, customization of the characters considered to be part of a word, temporary pop-up windows for buffer lists (and similar information), improved debugging information on procedure crashes, accommodations for formatting languages, and more.

MicroEMACS was begun by Dave Conroy in 1985, and then taken over by Daniel Lawrence (Lafayette, IN), who is still supporting and enhancing it. MicroEMACS is supported on a variety of machines and operating systems, including MS-DOS, VMS, and UNIX (several versions).

CUG 367 GNU File and Text Utilities for MS-DOS

CUG #367 introduces ports of various GNU file and text utilities to MS-DOS. These files are a variety of utilities derived from the GNU File Utilities. Thorsten Ohl was instrumental in porting these utilities to MS-DOS, with additional work by David J. MacKenzie, with help from Jim Meyering, Brian Mathews, Bruce Evans, and others. These files are part of the GNUish MS-DOS project. Sources, `man` files, and executables are included for `cat`, `chmod`, `cmp`, `cp`, `cut`, `dd`, `dir`, `head`, `ls`, `mkdir`, `mv`, `paste`, `rm`, `rmdir`, `tac`, `tail`, and `touch`. Source is also included for `du`. The routines are somewhat POSIX-compliant and at times improve on their UNIX counterparts in speed, options, and absence of arbitrary limits.

CUG 368   GNUlib for MS-DOS

CUG #368 provides a library of GNU library routines and other support routines for MS-DOS, ported by Thorsten Ohl. Files include `error.c`, `getopt.c`, `getopt.h`, `getopt1.c`, `glob.c`, `regex.c`, and `regex.h`. These are general-purpose routines needed by almost all GNU programs. These files are identical to or derived from versions distributed with the file utilities (CUG #367). `patches` can be used to recover original versions. `_cwild.c` provides command-line expansion, while `ndir.c` and `ndir.h` provide portable directory access. Other files include `pwd.c`, `pwd.h`, `gnulib.h` (some prototypes), `xmalloc.c`, `xrealloc.c`. The library would benefit from, but doesn't include, a version of the `obstack` macros for all memory models.

CUG 369   Genitor: Genetic Algorithm Tool

Contributed by Darrell Whitely. CUG #369 provides the Genitor genetic algorithm tool, produced by Darrell Whitley and his team at Colorado State University. Genetic algorithms solve problems with only a "genetic" code that defines the solution space and some measure of fitness of possible solutions represented by specific code. Genitor was designed for UNIX, but should port to other systems with a C compiler. The package comes from a graduate research environment. It assumes a knowledgeable user, documentation is sparse, and the package is not user-friendly. Genitor includes commented examples for traditional binary optimization, the Traveling Salesman Problem, and a neural net for solving the two-bit adder problem.

CUG 370   GATool: Genetic Algorithm Tool

Contributed by Sara Lienau. CUG #370 GATool brings a new genetic algorithm tool to the public domain, and can produce programs for applications. Genetic algorithms solve problems with only a "genetic" code describing the possible solutions and some measure of "fitness" of specific code solutions. GATool, an extensible, object-oriented C++ system, was written by Sara Lienau in a graduate research environment, so it assumes knowledgeable users and documentation is sparse. Designed for UNIX, it should be portable to other systems, but its menu-driven interface based on curses will cause some difficulty.

CUG 371   WindosIO: DLL for Console-Style I/O in a Window

WindosIO v2.0, CUG #371, is a shareware Dynamic Link Library
(DLL) for Microsoft Windows that supports both text and graphics I/O
so that programs can readily be ported from MS-DOS, in some cases
without change. Jeff Graubert-Cervone (Chicago, IL) is the author of
WinDosIO. WinDosIO v2.0 provides over 200 functions for standard
terminal-style I/O and Borland/Microsoft graphics under Microsoft
Windows 3.0 and 3.1, along with an online user manual, a reference
guide, and several example programs. WindosIO must be used with a
compiler that includes the Windows Software Development Toolkit.
The volume includes an import library, but not the source for the DLL.

CUG 372   Mouse++, String++, and Z++ (Complex Num) Classes

The Mouse++, String++, and Z++ classes, CUG #372, were written
by Carl Moreland, (Greensboro, NC), an electronics engineer who de-
signs microelectronic circuits and uses C, C++, and AWK. The classes
were developed for Borland C++ or Turbo C++. Mouse++ provides a
mouse-interface class and includes the ability to change the cursor.
Most of the standard mouse functions place their results directly into
class variables and return void. The values are obtained using the appropriate inline accessor functions for the private variables. String++
is a string class (v2.01) and Z++ (v1.0) is a complex-number class.
Moreland is developing a keyboard class that replaces the standard interrupt 9 handler and provides some unique mapping features. The
classes include excellent documentation and example programs.

CUG 373   MicroEMACS for Windows

MicroEMACS for Windows CUG #373 ports the popular Micro-
EMACS program to the Microsoft Windows environment. Micro-
EMACS was written by Daniel Lawrence (Lafayette, IN), based on
code by Dave Conroy, and ported to Windows by Pierre Perret (Glen-
dale, AZ). MicroEMACS for Windows is a port of MicroEmacs
v3.11c. Although MicroEMACS normally comes with documentation
and scripts (macros or MicroEMACS v3.11c command files, they are
not supplied with MicroEMACS for Windows, but are available with
MicroEMACS (CUG #366). Exhaustive online documentation (in
Winhelp format) is in the works and will be incorporated in this volume as soon as it is available.

Pierre Perret said that his port to Windows will become part of the next major release of MicroEMACS. The port was designed to preserve as much of MicroEMACS style as possible, to minimize changes to the core code. MicroEMACS calls "screens" what really should be called "MDI Windows" and calls "windows" what should be called "panes." Due to MicroEMACS heritage, various operations are definitely not CUA-compliant. The CUA.CMD file included with this package, loaded by the included EMACS.RC, contains macros that modify the standard MicroEMACS mouse bindings to provide a CUA-like interface. The combination of multiple screens with menus (which thoughtfully display the corresponding keystroke commands as shortcut key combinations) makes EMACS more accessible to beginners while maintaining its utility for experienced users. These release notes were prepared using MicroEMACS for Windows.

CUG 374 MicroSpell: Multiplatform Spell-Checker

MicroSpell v2.0, CUG #374 (formerly volume #248), provides a major release of Daniel Lawrence's (Lafayette, IN) spelling-checker program, which can be used as stand-alone or in conjunction with MicroEMACS v3.11. MicroSPELL has a 1,000-word common word list, a 67,000-word main dictionary, and can access multiple user dictionaries during a spell check. MicroSPELL runs under MS-DOS, with versions available for Amiga, Atari, several flavors of UNIX, and CMS on IBM 370s. MicroSPELL can be used with the MicroEMACS macro (scan.cmd) that scans text, stopping at suspect words and providing alternatives to deal with the word. Three utilities are included: DMERGE, for merging a text file of words and the main compressed dictionary; CDICT, for compressing a text dictionary; and BIC, for suggesting replacements for a suspect word. This volume replaces CUG #248, v1.0 of MicroSPELL. This volume includes sources, executables (for MS-DOS), dictionaries, and users' guide (in various formats).

CUG 375 TextView: DLL Simplifies Text Windows

TextView, CUG #375, is a free Dynamic Link Library (DLL) for simplified manipulation of text windows under Microsoft Windows, written by Alan Phillips (Lancaster, U.K.). Alan Phillips is a systems programmer at the Lancaster University Computer Centre, where he writes UNIX communications software.

Similar to WinDosIO (CUG #371), TextView handles the details of window operations, permitting users to call functions for writing text (such as TVOutputText) in much the same way printf would be called in an MS-DOS application (with the exception of an extra parameter to identify the window where the text will be written). TextView can create multiple, independent windows that can be resized, minimized, maximized, and scrolled horizontally and vertically. A thoroughly documented demonstration program illustrates the use of TextView windows to provide tracing and debugging information during application development. TextView requires the use of a compiler (such as Microsoft C) that can generate Windows code. The TextView volume includes a readable and carefully organized 42-page manual. The TextView functions follow the same conventions as the Windows API, and the manual uses the same layout as the *Microsoft Windows Programmer's Reference*. TextView function names all begin with TV. The functions use Pascal calling conventions and must be declared FAR.

Function prototypes are contained in the file textview.h. Adding this file to your source selects the right calling mode and performs necessary casts to far pointers. The TextView import library textview.lib must be included in the list of libraries to be linked. The stack size required for your application may need to be increased. Some functions in the TextView import library must be statically linked.

Support Resources

e-mail: a.phillips@lancaster.ac.uk

CUG 376 UNIX Tools for OS/2 and MS-DOS

CUG volume #376 adds OS/2 tools to the CUG library. Martii Ylikoski (Helsinki, Finland), has provided a large number of free, dualmode tools that support both OS/2 and MS-DOS. The tools are remarkably well packaged. Each tool includes accompanying source, makefile, documentation, and demo files, along with files (.bat or .cmd) to install and uninstall the tools. For OS/2 there is also a tools2.inf file, in the standard format for OS/2 help files. Full source code is included, generally with a single file per utility. The makefiles (toolname.mak) indicate the required dependencies. A library was used in building the tools, and is included in two forms: mtoolsp.lib for protected mode and mtoolsr.lib for real mode. No documentation for the libraries exists, other than the examples of function use provided in the source code for the tools. The collection of 54 utilities provides a variety of functions such as find file (ff), disk usage (du), head, tail, set priority (setprty), touch, cat, and scan (a find-like utility that searches for files and executes commands once the files are found).

CUG 377 DSR: Hard-to-Find Information on Floppy Disks

Diskette manipulations are the core of CUG #377, provided by Ian Ashdown, (West Vancouver). This volume provides a wealth of information about diskette device-service routine (DSR) functions. The documentation addresses a variety of quirks in diskette access, and provides considerable hard-to-find information on floppy diskettes, diskette controllers, and the diskette DSR functions. The volume also provides extensive example and test routines, with source code (in both C and C++ versions), for reading, writing, formatting, and verifying almost any IBM System 34 format diskette on a PC compatible. The code includes support and interface functions that increase the diskette DSR's reliability and provide a consistent programming interface across PC platforms. The information was largely determined through extensive use of an in-circuit emulator and other debugging tools, along with careful study of various machines and various DOS and BIOS versions. Given the variety of ROM BIOSs available, and the need to derive the information by experimentation, the material in this volume cannot cover every case, but it certainly provides a thorough and careful treatment.

CUG 378 NEWMAT: C++ Matrix Operations

From Robert Davies, a consultant and researcher in mathematics and computing from New Zealand, formerly with the New Zealand Department of Scientific and Industrial Research (DSIR), we get NEWMAT (CUG #378), a C++ matrix package. This volume was written for scientists and engineers who need to manipulate a variety of matrices using standard matrix operations. It was developed by a scientist to support real work. NEWMAT emphasizes operations supporting statistical calculations. Functions include least squares, linear-equation solve, and eigenvalues.

Matrix types supported include:

- Matrix (rectangular matrix)
- UpperTriangularMatrix

- LowerTriangularMatrix
- DiagonalMatrix
- SymmetricMatrix
- BandMatrix
- UpperBandMatrix
- LowerBandMatrix
- SymmetricBandMatrix
- RowVector
- ColumnVector

In keeping with object-oriented design, each type is derived from Matrix. Only one element type (float or double) is supported. Supported matrix operations include: *, +, ", inverse, transpose, conversion between types, submatrix, determinant, Cholesky decompositions, Householder triangularization, singular value decomposition, eigenvalues of a symmetric matrix, sorting, fast Fourier transform, printing, and an interface compatible with *Numerical Recipes in C*. NEWMAT supports matrices in the range of 4x4 to the machine-dependent, maximum array size 90x90 double elements, or 125x125 float elements for machines that have a limit for contiguous arrays of 64Kb. NEWMAT works for very small matrices, but is rather inefficient.

NEWMAT works with Borland and Glockenspiel C++. Robert Davies suggests the following as criteria for interest in NEWMAT: first, a desire for matrix operations expressed as operators; second, a need for various matrix types; third, a need for only a single element type; fourth, use of matrix sizes between 4x4 and 90x90; and fifth, tolerance for a large and complex package. There is a fairly large file documenting the package, which broadly addresses issues from particulars of functions and interactions with various compilers through design issues in building a matrix package. If you fit the profile described, then NEWMAT may be the matrix tool you need.

CUG 379   Zoo: Portable File Compression

ZOO v2.1, is a file archiving and compression program (standard extension .zoo), written by Rahul Dhesi, with assistance from J. Brian Walters, Paul Homchick, Bill Davidsen, Mark Alexander, Haruhiko Okumura, Randal L. Barnes, Raymond D. Gardner, Greg Yachuk, and Andre Van Dalen. This volume includes C source, executable, and documentation. Zoo is used to create and maintain collections of files in compressed form. It uses the Lempel-Ziv compression algorithm, which yields space savings from 20 percent to 80 percent depending on the file data. Zoo can manage multiple generations of the same file and has numerous options accompanied by lengthy descriptions in the manuals. Zoo supports a range of hardware and operating systems, and includes makefiles with various options. Zoo is part of the GNUish MS-DOS project, an attempt to provide a GNU-like environment for MS-DOS, with GNU ports and MS-DOS replacements for non-ported GNU software.

CUG 380   JMODEM: File Transfer Protocol

JMODEM, by Richard B. Johnson (Beverly, MA), is the definitive version of this innovative file transfer protocol. Johnson wrote and distributed the first version JMODEM protocol in 1989. Although originally written totally in assembler, he has since rewritten it in C and made the source freely available. His hope is that it will "make it easier for software developers throughout the world to use this very useful protocol."

The CUG volume includes a pre-built JMODEM MS-DOS executable that can be used as is. Much care has been taken to ensure that it behaves well as an externally shelled communications protocol driver. As such, you may simply add it to your existing upload/download protocol menu in Procomm, Telix, Commo, and other terminal programs. JMODEM also provides detailed installation instructions for BBS use. Developers of their own communications programs can also integrate JMODEM support. JMODEM requires as little as 79Kb RAM to run and can be built without any floating-point support libraries. The current version runs only on MS-DOS and has been successfully built with Microsoft C and Borland Turbo C.

You might ask why the world needs another file transfer protocol. JMODEM provides more intelligent block sizing, data compression, and CRC support than other file transfer protocols. Many of the older protocols, such as XMODEM and YMODEM variants, were designed when 1200 baud was state-of-the-art. As such, they use fairly small block sizes, which typically range from 128 to 1024 bytes in length. After each block gets transmitted, the older protocols require an immediate acknowledgement before any more data will be sent. The acknowledgement overhead and block size limitations together slow transmission down to 25 percent less than its maximum throughput.

JMODEM avoids the block size and acknowledgement logjam by allowing block sizes to increase to 8,192 bytes in length. JMODEM starts out the block size at 512 bytes in length. With each successively correct transmission, it doubles the block size to 1,024, 2,048, 4,096, and finally 8,192 bytes. Similarly, each successively incorrect transmission causes it to halve the previous block size. Block sizes as small as 64 bytes allow transmission even in a high-noise environment.

JMODEM remains one of the few file transfer protocols with built-in data compression. Specifically, JMODEM will provide Run-Length Encoding (RLE) on blocks in which an efficiency can be obtained. In pre-compressed data scenarios, such as the transmission of ZIP-ed files, JMODEM automatically disables its compression. Realistically, RLE can significantly help out older 2400 baud (v.22bis) modems on uncompressed data. However, RLE cannot beat modern hardware implemented compression protocols such as Microcom Networking Protocol (MNP 5) and the CCITT v.42bis LZW compression. MNP 5 typically achieves 2:1 compression and v.42bis achieves 4:1 compression.

Last, JMODEM provides a 16-bit cyclic redundancy check (CRC) for further protection against transmission errors. Older protocols, such as XMODEM, often rely on Checksums to guard against accidental transmission errors. Some protocols, such as ZMODEM, offer even higher protection via 32-bit CRCs. However, the 16-bit CRC means that only about 1 in 2^{132} errors will go undetected.

CUG 381 JPEG: Highly Portable Graphics Compression

JPEG Software, by Thomas G. Lane (The Independent JPEG Group), is a complete JPEG image compression and decompression system. JPEG (pronounced "jay-peg") is a standardized compression method for full-color and gray-scale images. JPEG originated from a desire to handle photographic images efficiently. The source of the image can be any sort of computer-captured or -generated medium, such as 35mm film scanners, video capture boards, or fractal landscapes.

The JPEG Software volume source code is written entirely in C. You can compile it on many platforms, including IBM compatibles, Amiga, Macintosh, Atari ST, DEC VAX/VMS, Cray Y/MP, and most UNIX platforms. Supported UNIX platforms include, but are not limited to, Apollo, HP-UX, SGI Indigo, and SUN Sparcstation. The make system even includes a utility to convert the ANSI-style C code back to older K&R style.

JPEG differs considerably from file formats such as PCX, GIF, and TIFF, which must reproduce 100 percent of the original image data. Rather, JPEG is said to be "lossy" in that that the output image is not necessarily identical to the input image. Applications requiring exact correspondence between input and output bits, such as engineering blueprints, are thus inappropriate for JPEG. However, on typical photographic images, JPEG delivers very good compression levels without visible change. Additionally, amazingly high compression is possible if you can tolerate a low-quality image. You can trade off image quality against file size by adjusting the compressor's "quality" setting.

By default, the JPEG Software volume builds a command-line driven translator. The currently supported image file formats are PPM (PBMPLUS color format), PGM (PBMPLUS gray-scale format), GIF, Targa, and RLE (Utah Raster Toolkit format). RLE is supported only if the URT library is available. The compression program `cjpeg` recognizes the input image format automatically, with the exception of some Targa-format files. Of course for the decompression program `djpeg`, you have to tell it what file format to generate. The only JPEG file format currently supported is the JFIF format. Support for the TIFF 6.0 JPEG format will probably be added at some future date.

You may incorporate any or all of the JPEG Software source code into your own applications. The only restriction is that you must include a small notice, stating "This software is based in part on the work of the Independent JPEG Group."

Support Resources

WWW: `http://www.ijg.org`

CUG 382   GZIP: Highly Portable File Compression

GZIP, by Jean-Loup Gailly (Rueil-Malmaison, France), is a general-purpose archiving and compression utility. Rather than introducing yet another compression file format, GZIP seeks to unite the existing myriad compression methods. Specifically, GZIP will automatically detect and uncompress files created by Phil Katz PKZIP and compatible zip methods. It also handles UNIX-derived "pack" (Huffman encoding) and "compress" (LZW) files.

GZIP v1.0.7 (released 3/18/93) supports many platforms, including MS-DOS, OS/2, Atari, Amiga, and DEC VAX/VMS. GZIP works well with most UNIX workstations, including those compatible with NeXT, MIPS, SGI Indigo, and Sun Sparcstations. On the MS-DOS platform, GZIP guarantees to work only with Microsoft C 5.0 (or later) and Borland Turbo C 2.0 (or later). By default, GZIP builds for the MS-DOS

Compact memory model. An additional compilation flag allows for large memory model. Other memory model variations might possibly be used as well, though only the small model is specifically disclaimed.

GZIP uses the well-known Lempel-Ziv encoding method as published in the *IEEE Transactions on Information Theory* (1977). As such, it avoids the patented algorithms that prevail in many implementations. Typical text, such as English or C source code, reduces in size about 60 to 70 percent. Files that are already signficantly compressed, such as GIF graphics and VOC audio files, undergo far less reduction. The algorithm itself is implemented entirely in C — with one exception: The routines that do the performance-critical, longest-string matching have been rewritten in platform-specific assembly language.

GZIP is licensed under the GNU General Public Software License. This means that if you plan on incorporating source code from GZIP in your own product, you must make source code readily available. However, you are still free to distribute the unmodified version of GZIP and bundle files archived with it.

CUG 383   VGL: 256-Color VGA Graphics Library

The VGL graphics library, by Mark Morley (Victoria, B.C., Canada), is a complete graphics library for use with VGA mode 13H. As you may recall, when IBM first introduced the VGA in 1987, the revolutionary 320x200 resolution with 256 colors (mode 13H) was one of its biggest improvements over the EGA. As was typical of IBM PC hardware, the VGA did not include any programming tools. Freeware programming tools, such as the VGL graphics library, help fill the void for DOS programmers. The VGL graphics library includes routines for drawing on virtual screens, drawing sprites, doing fast blits, animating the palette, drawing bitmapped fonts, loading GIF images, drawing lines, trapping keypresses, and even mouse handling. VGL v2.0, released on 5/93, is available as volume #383 in the CUG Library.

Above all, the VGL graphics library is fast. Animation appeared quite smooth even with my pokey old 386–20MHz CPU. Morley maximizes speed by writing about one-third of the package in hand-optimized assembly language. The core routines even appear in separate versions for 80286 and 80386 CPUs. The 80386 version takes advantage of 32-bit registers, such as EAX, and their instruction extensions. With its speed of animation, VGL graphics makes a great starting base for game programming.

VGL includes 22 fonts for serious work and fun work. For serious applications, Helvetica (from 13 to 29 points) and Times Roman (12 or 14 points) look great. For fun applications, there are cartoon, comics, stencil, art deco, and other fonts. VGL renders fonts in regular, under-lined, boldface, italics, and shadowed attributes as desired. Of course, the font displays are fast too.

CUG 384   Ghostscript: A PostScript Previewer

Ghostscript, by L. Peter Deutsch of Aladdin Enterprises (Menlo Park, CA), consists of an Adobe Postscript ™ compatible interpreter, fonts, and utilities. The interpreter is composed of C functions that im-plement the graphics capabilities that appear as primitive operations in the PostScript language. Ghostscript interprets your PostScript files and can print to a variety of displays, printers, and graphics file for-mats. Ghostscript v2.6.1 is available as CUG volume #384.

For example, you can view the PostScript files on EGA, VGA, and many SuperVGAs. You can print the files to an HP LaserJet (LJ), LJ+, LJ IIp, LJ III, DeskJet (color or mono), PaintJet, IBM ProPrinter, Epson, and other printers. Ghostscript will write out to mono or 256-color GIF files as well as mono, 16-color, or 256-color PC Paintbrush (.PCX) files.

Ghostscript will work on any PC with EGA (or better) graphics and MS-DOS v3.1 (or later). You may also build Ghostscript as a Windows 3.0 or 3.1 application. Ghostscript runs on most UNIX systems, in-cluding Sun Sparcstations, SCO UNIX, DECStation and VAX Ultrix, SGI Iris Indigo, Sequent, and more. The CUG Library edition of Ghostscript includes pre-built versions for MS-Windows and DOS only. The DOS version must be built with a DOS Extender such as DOS/4GW by Rational Systems, Inc.

Ghostscript includes many useful PostScript fonts. Most fonts are derivatives of the public domain Hershey and MIT X11 distribution. These fonts include Avante-Garde, Bookman, Courier, Helvetica, New Century Schoolbook, Palatino, Times-Roman, Zapf Chancery, and many more.

Ghostscript is licensed under the GNU General Public Software Li-cense. This means that if you plan on incorporating source code from Ghostscript in your own product, you must make source code readily available. However, you are still free to distribute the unmodified ver-sion of Ghostscript and bundle files archived with it.

CUG 385   BCC+ TSR, DOSThread, and Coroutine Classes

From John English, at the University of Brighton (England), comes a trilogy of highly useful class libraries for Borland C++. The TSR class presents a framework for writing memory-resident DOS programs (TSRs). The DOSThread class presents a framework for writing DOS applications consisting of multiple threads in a self-contained preemptive multitasker. The Coroutine class presents a cooperative non-premptive framework for sharing the CPU. Version 1.00 (March 1993) of all three BCC+ class libraries is available as CUG Library volume #385.

CUG 385A   TSR Class for Borland C++

After more than a decade of MS-DOS, resident programs remain as tricky as ever to design and implement properly. If anything, writing TSRs becomes more complex with every new version of MS-DOS, Windows, and other environments. The TSR class helps make development of resident programs an attainable goal for Borland C++ programs. Applications developed with TSR class require an 80286 (or better) and DOS v3.1 (or later) on the target machine. Building them requires Borland C++ v3.0 (or later).

TSRs produced using this class can be woken up by a specific key (the hotkey), or after a specified number of timer ticks (the timeslice), or a combination of both. You must supply a function main in your application class to be invoked whenever the TSR is woken up. The member function run makes the TSR resident. The member function loaded tells whether an instance is already resident. The member function unload can then remove it. A foreground copy can also communicate with a resident copy using the functions request and respond. Each TSR must be given a unique name up to 32 characters long.

CUG 385B   DOSThread Class for Borland C++

MS-DOS remains a single-threaded operating system, even with today's most advanced version. Many of the functions in its published interrupt API are non-reentrant. However, the DOSThread class lets you create multithreaded DOS applications with ease. Like the aforementioned TSR class, the DOSThread class requires a main function, which gets invoked by the member function run.

Once started, each thread runs in a single timer tick (55 ms) interval before being preempted by the scheduler. Intervals can be set for any integral number of ticks by the timeslice member function. Alternately, scheduling can be disabled, thus providing non-preemptive multitasking. Threads can put themselves to sleep with the wait member function, yield control with the pause member function, and kill any thread with the terminate member function. The extra classes DOSMonitor and DOSMonitorQueue provide monitor classes for intertask communication. A monitor contains data structures that can be accessed by several threads.

CUG 385C   Coroutine Class for Borland C++

The Coroutine class is similar to the DOSThread class except that it is always a cooperative multitasker. The Coroutine class has some elements in common with the TSR and DOSThread classes. Once again, the Coroutine class requires a main function, which gets invoked by the member function run. Since coroutines are non-preemptive by definition, the other member function needed is pause to yield control. Synchronization is unnecessary because coroutines never interrupt each other.

CUG 386   Thomson-Davis Editor

The Thomson-Davis Editor, as provided by Frank Davis (Tifton, GA), is a multi-file/multi-window binary and text file editor written for IBM PCs and close compatibles. Thomson-Davis Editor (TDE) works well with batch files, binary files, text files, and various computer language source code files. TDE can handle any size of file and any number of windows that fit in conventional DOS memory. Davis's most recent improvement is support for regular expressions in searching text and selecting files for editing. TDE v3.0 (June 1993) is available as CUG Library volume #386.

The TDE compiles under Microsoft C v5.1 through v7.0 as well as QuickC v2.5. TDE also supports Borland C v3.1. The same makefile can be used with either Microsoft nmake or Borland make utilities. Assembly language portions will build with Microsoft MASM 5.1 through 6.0, Quick Assembler, or Borland Turbo Assembler. The CUG Library volume also includes a complete compiled and linked TDE.EXE.

TDE includes more than 800Kb of C source code plus two small modules in Assembler (26Kb). The TDE source code itself is remarkably well documented. Each function includes a detailed header describing parameters and purpose of the function. Best of all, TDE provides an incredible amount of detail in bibliographic references to algorithms employed. For example, the sort.c module provides precise references to all of C.A.R. Hoare original work on QuickSort (1961) plus embellishments by Knuth and Sedgewick. Overall, the references remain current and even include information accurately reflecting changes in MS-DOS v6.0.

Since the TDE has been officially released into the public domain, you may use and distribute it freely. There is no copyright, no fee for use, no licensing, and no registration. This editor is not user-supported, corporate-sponsored, or government-subsidized — it is sustained and maintained solely by Frank Davis.

CUG 387   C/C++ Lost Algorithms

The C/C++ Lost Algorithms, by John Tal (Rochester, MI), releases handy implementations of textbook classic algorithms into the public domain. These algorithms are implemented twice (once in C and again in C++) and focus primarily on Link Lists, Binary Trees, Stacks, FIFO Queues, and Heaps (Priority Queues). He places secondary importances on algorithms for Shell sort, file merging, multitasking and processing scheduling, Virtual Memory Management, file-based process communication, graph/network job management, and data encryption. The algorithms (as released in Fall 1992) are available as CUG #393.

Tal expresses concern that many of the world's best and most efficient algorithms have been carelessly disregarded in the wake of faster computers with more memory. He points out that it will *always* make sense to make the best use of any computing resource.

The C/C++ Lost Algorithms have been tested on a variety of platforms including both DOS, OS/2, and UNIX workstations. Each algorithm set includes complete documentation in the form of a UNIX-style man page. The C++ implementation includes general porting notes and Borland Turbo C++ .prj makefiles. As an added bonus, Tal also includes implementations of UNIX utilities binsrch (binary search on flat file), cat, db (dump bytes), split, tail, and wc (word count).

CUG 388   Anthony's Tools: Editor, make, grep, and Stdscr Curses

Anthony C. Howe (Waterloo, Ontario) presents his award-winning Editor, make, grep, and Stdscr Curses tools. Anthony's Tools have won the International Obfuscated C Code Contest (IOCCC) for Best Utility in 1990, 1992, and 1993 respectively. For those who are unfamiliar with it, the IOCCC competition pits C programmers against each other to see who can produce the most unreadable and obscure code that compiles and runs. Fortunately, he has included both the obfuscated and readable source versions of each utility. Both versions of all tools have been listed as public domain, except for the readable version of Anthony's Editor, which remains freeware. All of Anthony's Tools are available on CUG volume #388.

Anthony's Editor appears in both its obfuscated 1991 award-winning form and its readable July 1993 version. Both versions will compile and run on PCs and UNIX workstations. The 1993 version of Anthony's Editor (AE) can be configured for modal (vi-style) or modeless (EMACS-style) user interface. The configuration file also presents the key mapping for each internal command. Thus, you can customize AE to your preferences or support any conceivable terminal. AE can edit arbitrarily long lines of text and assumes tabstops every eight characters. AE includes cut, copy, and paste operations with blocks of text. The same buffer is also used for a single-level undo command. The AE macro facility allows one keystroke to feed other keystrokes into the buffer and execute them. AE does not provide any searching or replacing operations.

Anthony's Make provides most of the functionality required of make utilities under POSIX.2 draft standard 11.2. Indeed, the judges were so impressed as to jokingly recommend lobbying the IEEE for an obfuscated POSIX subcommittee. Anthony's Make (AM) has been tested with GCC under SunOS, Sozobon C on Atari ST, Borland Turbo C on PCs, and Interactive UNIX System V/386 Release 3.2. On the PC, the AM executable is less than 18Kb in size! AM supports many of the constructs you've come to expect in makefiles, including macros, multiple targets and dependencies, comments, and more.

Anthony's Grep provides most of the POSIX.2 functionality for grep utilities. Anthony's Grep (AG) can be built on the same platforms as AM plus WatCom C for the PC. AG supports a useful subset of POSIX.2 Extended Regular Expressions (ERE). It has a recursive ERE parser/compiler that generates an NFA railroad. AG uses lazy NFA to DFA evaluation to improve performance speed. AG is both useful and useable for a variety of applications.

Anthony's Stdscr Curses is the only one of these tools that is limited to PC platforms. Anthony calls it quick and dirty because it assumes that only stdscr is used and therefore goes directly to BIOS rather than waiting for a refresh(). Unlike the other modules, Stdscr Curses doesn't include formal documentation, so a working knowledge of UNIX curses is essential.

CUG 389   VGA FontLib, MakeFont, and CDXF Viewer

Joseph V. Gagliano (Austin, TX) submits a pair of utilities developing MS-DOS applications with VGA graphics fonts and a stand-alone DXF (AutoCAD vector) viewer. FontLib is a set of 13 functions for rendering fonts on EGA and VGA displays with a minimum of resolution of at least 640x350. MakeFont is an editor for producing and editing your own font files. CDXF views 2-D AutoCAD-compatible vector files and is not a development tool. All three are marketed as shareware and require separate registration with the author after an evaluation period. The latest versions of all three (released 09/16/93) are available as CUG #389.

FontLib comes with small model library built with Microsoft QuickC v2.5. FontLib currently does not claim compatability with any other compilers. Registration of FontLib for $25 includes the full library source code for the Microsoft compilers, unlimited technical support, and low-cost upgrades. Registration also grants you royalty-free use of the library functions. For an additional $10, you receive source code to MakeFont as well.

FontLib characters can be rendered in normal or boldface, in different colors, vertically or horizontally, and with shadowing effects. You can embed style-rendering changes in a string using escape codes to make color and shadowing changes within the context of a single string display call. The baker's dozen of functions appears below:

Function Name	Purpose
regfont();	Load the font for immediate use
draw_letter();	Display a single character
draw_letter_bold();	As above, in boldface
letter();	Display entire string
letter_bold();	As above, in boldface
letter_w();	Display string using window coords
letter_bold_w();	As above, in boldface
letter_column();	Display string as vertical column
letter_column_bold();	As above, in boldface
letter_column_w();	With window coords
letter_column_bold_w();	And in boldface

```
freefont();                      Unload the font
set_shadow_color();              Use this color for shadowing effect
set_font_color();                Use this color for base colors
```

The CUG volume includes four font files: 8x5, 13x8, 20x12, and 20x20 characters. The following figure shows MakeFont editing the letter "V" in the 20x20 font. The font file format is plain ASCII and is well documented in the 20-page reference manual in this volume. FontLib and MakeFont work only with monospaced raster font files.

As mentioned earlier, CDXF currently does not have any source code availability. CDXF requires a $25 registration for the first copy and $5 for every copy thereafter.

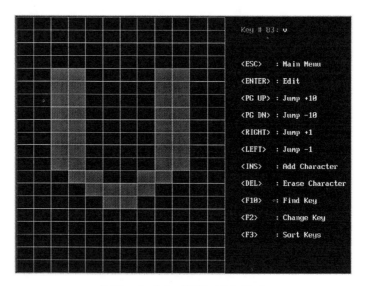

Editing the letter "V" in MakeFont

CUG 390   ACTLIB: Another C Tools LIB

Marc Stern of S. A. Philips Industrial and Telecommunication Systems (Brussels, Belgium) presents Another C Tools Library (ACTLIB) for MS-DOS developers. ACTLIB contains tricks and algorithms that will be very helpful for novice MS-DOS C programmers. There are also some things for advanced C programmers as well. These low-level disk and keyboard functions answer many frequently asked questions. The string and date function library should work on a broader base of platforms. ACTLIB v1.4 (released 05/27/93) is available as CUG #390.

ACTLIB has been compiled and tested using Borland C 3.1 and Microsoft C 7.0. The only assembly language file is one that supplies a function to return the CPU type. No makefiles are included with the library. The TOOLS.LIB library provides the low-level functions specific to MS-DOS, including:

- get return value of previously executed program;
- get extended keyboard keys (F1,... Alt-X,...);
- put a key back into keyboard buffer;
- open more than 20 files;
- get the density of a floppy drive;
- test the availability of a drive (exists, formatted,...);
- very fast file copy;
- very fast multiple files deletion;
- input a password;
- get/set disk volume label;
- get CPU type (86, 186, 286, 386, 486); and
- disallow debugging of your program.

The STRINGS.LIB library provides 28 source files of functions to simplify common string-handling tasks. These functions perform complex operations such as regular expression handling via recursion, string mathematical expression evaluation (e.g., 1 + 2 * 3/4), and multiple substring replacement. Simpler functions perform BASIC-like left, right, and mid string extractions. Functions such as these can help out nearly any application.

The DATE.LIB library provides functions to validate dates, perform simple date arithmetic, and answer the question "What day of the week is it?".

CUG 391   C/C++ Exploration Tools

C/C++ Exploration Tools, by Juergen Mueller (Kornwestheim, Germany), includes both his C Function Tree Generator (CFT) and the C Structure Tree Generator (CST). CFT and CST analyze the C/C++ source code of applications of any size with multiple files. CFT and CST are useful to explore new, unknown software and to support reuse, maintenance, and re-engineering. By preprocessing, scanning, and analyzing the program source code, these programs generate the function call hierarchy (CFT) and the data structure/class (CST) relations. Both programs can handle C and C++ code; CFT can also analyze assembler code. The C Exploration Tools v2.12 as MS-DOS executables (released 07/03/93) are available as CUG volume #391.

An important feature of C Exploration Tools is the database generation that allows the recalling of informations without reprocessing the source. This database can again be read from CFT and CST to produce different outputs or to add new files to the database. The database format is dBASE-compatible. Special recall programs called CFTN and CSTN allow fast searching for items in the database. These programs can be used within any environment — for example, from inside editors such as BRIEF, QEDIT, or MicroEMACS (DOS and Windows version), to provide a full software project management system with access to all functions and data types with just a keystroke. This feature makes a comfortable "hypertext source code browser and locator" system out of the editor.

The documentation is supplied in ASCII and includes 63 pages of reference material. The manual is in plain English and should be accessible to even novice C programmers, even though advanced techniques are discussed.

The C Exploration Tools are shareware and require registration with the author if you decide to use them beyond the 30-day evaluation period. The registration price is $46 U.S. or 60 DM for a single copy. Generous site license discounts with prices as low as $15 are appropriate for corporate use or educational institutions. Registered users automatically receive Protected Mode versions of the tools optimized for 80386 and the latest versions of everything. Source code for the C Exploration Tools itself is not available.

Related Volumes:

• C/C++ Exploration Tools for Windows (CUG #437)

CUG 392   GNU Indent: Beautifies Your C Code

GNU Indent, from Joseph Arceneaux (San Francisco, CA), becomes the newest installment of high-quality tools from GNU project. The Indent program changes the appearance of a C program by inserting or deleting whitespace. The Indent program can be used to make code easier to read. It can also convert from one style of writing C to another. Indent understands a substantial amount about the syntax of C, but it also attempts to cope with incomplete and misformed syntax. Indent can replace the original source .c file and retain a backup copy or else write its output to a new .c file. GNU Indent v1.8 (released 06/16/93) is available as CUG volume #392.

There are several common styles of C code, including the GNU style, the Kernighan & Ritchie style, and the original Berkeley style. A style may be selected with a single "background" option, which specifies a set of values for all other options. However, explicitly specified options always override options implied by a background option. Thus, you can create hybrid styles or a new coding style uniquely your own by combining the many option settings.

Option settings include many things that programmers regularly spar about, such as:

- Placement of blank lines, braces, and comments
- Special handling for braces around if/then/else constructs
- Spacing around casts and sizeof()
- Overall number of spaces per indentation level
- Alignment of parenthesis on continuation lines
- All aspects of function declaration layout

Each option can be specified in short form or long form. For example, the short form option -ncdb can be entered as --no-comment-delimiters-on-blank-lines.

GNU Indent supports MS-DOS, OS/2, VAX VMS, and most versions of UNIX. For UNIX versions, it includes the popular GNU autoconfiguration utility which customizes the Makefile to meet the needs of your system. The CUG Library volume includes source code only.

CUG 393   LL, GIFSave, and Cordic++

As you might have guessed from the introduction, this volume is something of a C potpourri. George Matas (University of Surrey, U.K.) presents his "LL" for a generic double-linked list library with examples. Sverre H. Huseby (Oslo, Norway) contributes "GIFSave" to save bitmaps in this popular image file format. Last, "Cordic++" by Timothy M. Farnum (Rochester, NY) builds on Michael Bertrand's C implementation of fast trigonometric functions. Altogether, three very useful and specialized tools for common C problems. This set is available as CUG volume #393.

CUG 393A   LL: Doubly-Linked List Handler Library

LL is a double-linked list handler library with more than four dozen operator functions. Variables of any type can be stored in an LL list. Individual elements of a list may be of different types. Any depth of lists of lists can be created. An instance of a list is created using either ConsLL(), ConsCopyLL() or ConsPtrLL() functions. Its best to call one of these functions at the point of declaration of a list variable. The result of one of the constructor functions must be assigned to a given list instance before passing it to any other function in the LL library.

ConsLL() creates an empty list. ConsCopyLL(src) creates a new copy of an existing list. ConsPtrLL(src) creates a list of pointers to elements stored in list src. DestLL(list) destroys a list, ie., deletes all elements and frees all memory allocated for list. It should be called at the point where list goes out of scope.

LL has been tested only on SUN Sparcstations and DEC Ultrix machines. In these environments, it works with both the native "cc" compiler as well as GNU C ("gcc"). The CUG Library volume includes source only.

CUG 393B   GIFSave: Save Bitmaps in .GIF Format

The GIFSAVE library makes it possible to save GIF-images from your own graphic-producing C-programs. GIFSAVE creates simple GIF-files following the GIF87a standard. Interlaced images can not be created, and there should only be one image per file. GIFSAVE has been released as Public Domain source code with no restrictions on its usage.

GIFSAVE consists of four functions, all decleared in GIFSAVE.H:

- GIF_Create() creates new GIF-files. It takes parameters specifying the filename, screen size, number of colors, and color resolution.
- GIF_SetColor() sets up the red, green and blue color components. It should be called once for each possible color.
- GIF_CompressImage() performs the compression of the image. It accepts parameters describing the position and size of the image on screen, and a user defined callback function that is supposed to fetch the pixel values.
- GIF_Close() terminates and closes the file.

The functions should be called in the listed order for each GIF-file. One file must be closed before a new one can be created. To use these functions, you must create a callback function that will do what is needed to get the pixel values for each point in the image.

GIFSAVE includes a makefile for use with Borland C/C++. Huseby claims he has taken care to ensure that all byte-order sensitive operations are handled in a platform-independent method. This means the source code should work without modification on non-MS-DOS platforms.

The Graphics Interchange Format© is the copyrighted property of CompuServe Incorporated. GIF™ is a Service Mark property of CompuServe Incorporated.

CUG 393C   CORDIC++: Fast Trig Function Class Library

The Coordinate Rotational Digital Computer (CORDIC) was an early device implementing fast integer sine and cosine calculations. By favoring integer operations over floating-point ones, it represents a classic computing tradeoff of speed versus precision. Although first documented by Jack E. Volder in 1959, you may remember Michael Bertrand's C implementation in *CUJ* Vol. 10, No. 11 (November 1992). Farnum presents his own reimplementation of Bertrand's code this time as a full C++ class.

According to Farnum, the most notable change for C++ is encapsulating the variables that were global in the C version. As static member variables of the cordic class, they become protected from accidental modification by routines unaware of them. Moving these variables inside a class structure makes it necessary to develop interface routines, and also requires that a decision be made about how the class will be used. Farnum decided to predefine one member of the cordic class, cord, to access the member functions that compute the integer sine and cosine. Other instances of the cordic class can be created and will work as well as the predefined instance, but there is little advantage to this in the current implementation.

One implementation possibility left open to other readers is providing the ability to instantiate the class with different levels of accuracy. This would be done by using different bases for the CORDIC algorithm. Farnum decided against that alternative because the complexity of implementation and its use seemed to go against the straightforwardness that is the main advantage of the CORDIC algorithm.

CUG 394   C++SIM: Discrete Simulations

The C++SIM discrete event process based simulation package provides Simula-style class libraries. C++SIM is a newly released package from M.C. Little and D. McCue at the Department of Computing Science in the University of Newcastle upon Tyne (England). The same volume also includes the SIMSET linked list manipulation facilities. According to MacLennan (1983), Simula was the first computer language to incorporate the ideas of a "class" and "object" constructs, in 1967. SIM++ currently claims usability only on UNIX workstations, such as SUN Sparcs. C++SIM v1.0 (released 06/15/92) is available as CUG volume #394.

C++SIM uses inheritance throughout the design to an even greater extent than already provided by Simula. This allows adding new functionality without affecting the overall system structure. Thus, inheritance provides for a more flexible and expandable simulation package. Specifically, C++SIM supports the following classes: `Process`, `ProcessList`, `ProcessIterator`, `ProcessCons`, `Random`, `Element` & `Head`, `thread`, `lwp_thread`, and `gnu_thread`.

C++SIM includes a paper describing its design and implementation and examples of how to use it. The paper describes the class hierarchy itself as well as how to further refine the simulation package. The simulation package requires a threads package and currently works only with either the Sun lightweight process library or the included GNU thread package. The thread library is the only system-specific code, so porting the remainder to other UNIX workstations should be easy. C++SIM compiles with Cfront v2.1, Cfront v3.0.1 and GNU g++ v2.3.3.

The C++SIM license grants permission to use, copy, modify, and distribute the program for evaluation, teaching, and/or research purposes only and without fee. The University of Newcastle upon Tyne copyright and permission notice must appear on all copies and supporting documentation, and similar conditions are imposed on any individual or organization to whom the program is distributed.

Support Resources

WWW: `http://cxxsim.ncl.ac.uk/homepage.html`

CUG 395   Input-Edit, SORTLIST AVL, and Typing Tutor

This volume combines three relatively small but powerful archives. Chris Thewalt (University of California at Berkeley, Civil Engineering) presents his interactive line editor library. Walter Karas (Cary, NC) contributes his implementation of the classic binary search tree with AVL balancing. Christopher Sawtell (Linwood, Christchurch, New Zealand) releases his Typing Tutor for use with Curses. All three are available as CUG volume #395.

CUG 395A   Input-Edit

Input-Edit, also known as getline, provides an easy method to greatly increase the functionality of programs that read input a line at a time. Interactive programs that read input line by line can now provide line-editing and history functionality to the end-user who runs the program. As far as the programmer is concerned, the program asks only for the next line of input. However, until the user presses the [RETURN] key, they can use EMACS-style-line editing commands and can traverse the history of lines previously typed.

Other packages, such as GNU's readline, have greater capability but are also substantially larger. Input-Edit is small (1200 source lines) and quite portable because it uses neither stdio nor any termcap features. For example, it uses only \b to backspace and \007 to ring the bell on errors. Since it cannot edit multiple lines, it scrolls long lines left and right on the same line.

Input-Edit uses K&R C and can run on any UNIX system (BSD, SYSV or POSIX), AIX, XENIX, MS-DOS with MSC, Borland Turbo C, or djgpp, OS/2 with gcc (EMX), and DEC VAX-11 VMS. Porting the package to new systems consists mainly of maintaining the function to read a character when it is typed without echoing it.

CUG 395B   SORTLIST AVL

SORTLIST v1.1 (released 8/25/93) implements a "sorted list" data structure library in ANSI C. This library is appropriate whenever all elements of the sorted list have the following characteristics:

1. All elements are of a single fixed size.
2. Each element is associated with a unique key value.
3. The set of key values has a well-defined, less than, greater than relation.

Symbol tables and dictionary applications are excellent candidates for the sorted list data structure. This implementation of a sorted list data structure employs an AVL tree. AVL trees were invented by Adelson-Velskii and Landis in 1962. Specifically, Karas draws on algorithms presented by Horowitz and Sahni in *Fundamentals of Data Structures*, Computer Science Press, 1983, Rockville, MD). The add, find, and delete operations on an AVL tree have worst-case O(log n) time complexity.

CUG 395C   Typing Tutor

The Typing Tutor for use with Curses is a marvel of compactness. Since it builds on the substantial functionality of the UNIX Curses library, the Typing Tutor consists of just 250 source lines. The learning scenario is simple, yet easily customizable to fit any lesson plan. The screen is broken into two windows. The top window contains the "lesson," which is the text from which you will be typing. The bottom window contains the results of your (presumably) touch typing. Everytime a character in the bottom window fails to match the original in the top window, it is flagged by changing the screen attribute to flashing. Although Sawtell does not specify compatability for Typing Tutor, he expects it to run on any UNIX system with a Curses package available.

CUG 396   NNUTILS: Neural Network

NNUTILS, by Gregory Stevens (Rochester, NY), is a public domain package meant to help you to start programming neural networks in C. It is a tutorial about how to program neural networks where source code is your textbook. Stevens's intensely documented source code contains everything you need to implement several kinds of net architectures. NNUTILS gives you a series of simple implementations to let you see how they work step by step. NNUTILS v1.01 (released 08/02/93) is available as CUG #396.

Each subdirectory contains a different example with six standard C source files and a main program with a name similar to that of the directory. The source is written ANSI-compliant C and developed primarily under Borland C++ v3.1. Accordingly, the CUG volume includes DOS executables and project files for each implementation. Because the code is ANSI compliant, all of the examples work with GNU C under UNIX. Building executables with GNU C is simple enough that no makefiles are included.

Briefly, here's a summary of problem sets included with NNUTILS:

NNTEST1	A network with one input node and one output node.
NNTEST2	A network using the "logistic" activation function (as opposed to linear).
NNXOR	A network implementation of the famous Exclusive Or problem.
NNSIM1	A generic feed-forward network with back propagation.

NNWHERE	A 5x5 retina is presented with shapes it must classify correctly.
NNWHAT	A continuation of above, where shapes can assume any position.
NNEVOLVE	A feed-forward, back-propagation supervised net.
NNSIM2	Simulates a competitive learning network with a Hebbian learning algorithm.
NNRECUR1	A recurrent net with back-propagation, a kind of supervised learning called Self-Correlating, where the input patterns serve as their own output patterns.

CUG 397   International Obfuscated C Code Contest 1984–1993

Landon Noll (Sunnyvale, CA) submits a decade of source code from the International Obfuscated C Code Contest (IOCCC). This contest has long been a favorite of many *CUJ* readers. The entire IOCCC archive from 1984–1993 is available as CUG volume #397. Obfuscation implies purposefully obscuring and confusing a situation. Why obfuscate C code? The official IOCCC rules state it succinctly:

- To write the most Obscure/Obfuscated C program under the rules.
- To show the importance of programming style, in an ironic way.
- To stress C compilers with unusual code.
- To illustrate some of the subtleties of the C language.
- To provide a safe forum for poor C code. : -)

Bob van der Poel reviewed Don Libes's book entitled "Obfuscated C and Other Mysteries" (see *C Users Journal*, Vol. 11, No. 10, October 1993, pp. 131–132). The companion CD-ROM at the back of this book includes IOCCC entries from 1984–1991. Libes has produced special reports about the IOCCC several times in the *CUJ*. Please see the following back issues for more detail:

Libes, Don. "Don't Put This on Your Resume," *C Users Journal*, May 1991, p. 89.

Libes, Don. "The Far Side of C," *C Users Journal*, May 1990, p. 125.

Libes, Don. "The International Obfuscated C Code Contest," *C Users Journal*, July 1989, p. 93.

The CUG Library volume #397 contains the full IOCCC archive including two additional years not included in the Libes book.

In addition to dozens and dozens of obfuscated C programs, the archive includes complete rules and guidelines so you can submit your own entries into next year's contest. Some of the obfuscated programs are quite useful, including scaled-down versions of make, grep, and editors.

CUG 398   ASxxxx Cross-Assembler — Part 3

Cross-assemblers continue to play an important role in the CUG Library. A cross-assembler reads assembly language source code for a non-native CPU and writes object code that can be linked and downloaded to the target machine for execution. Developers of embedded systems are the most frequent users of cross-assemblers. Alan R. Baldwin (Kent State University, OH), adds his third cross-assembler to the CUG Library's repetoire. ASxxx Part 3 provides a complete Motorola 68HC08 development system. ASxxx Part 3 v1.50 (released 8/9/93) is available as CUG volume #398.

The CUG volume of ASxxx Part 3 includes MS-DOS executables for the ASxxx Cross-Assembler and Linker. However, if you want to recompile the Cross-Assembler or Linker, you'll also need ASxxx Part 1 (CUG #292). ASxxx Part 2 contains cross-assembler source files for the 6816 CPU. The ASxxxx family of cross-assemblers can be built on DEC machines running DECUS C in the TSX+ environment or PDOS C v5.4b under RT-11. ASxxxx has been built with Borland C++ v3.1 under MS-DOS and includes a project (.PRJ) file. Although only these implementations have been specifically tested, Baldwin claims many other K&R C compilers may work as well.

ASxxx Part 3 includes a comprehensive 80-page manual covering functionality provided by all three existing ASxxxx cross-assemblers and linkers. The documentation lays out the exact specifications of syntax for symbols, labels, assembler directives, and expressions in detail. The manual includes appendixes with instruction set highlights and supported syntax for Motorola 6800, 6801, 6804, 6805, 68HC08, 6809, 6811, 6816; Intel 8080 and 8085; and Zilog Z80; and HD64180 CPUs.

The ASxxxx assembler falls short of full macro implementation, but does include a host of important features such as if/then/else, #include files, radix support from binary to hexadecimal, and a full complement of Clanguage operators for expressions. The ASxxxx linker goes beyond conventional loaders by resolving intermodule symbols, combining code into segments, relocating absolute symbols and base addresses, and producing either Intel HEX or Motorola S19 output files.

CUG 399 MINED: Multi-Platform Editor

MINED, by Thomas Wolff (Germany), is a modeless full-screen text editor. MINED was originally written for MINIX and now works with most UNIX platforms as well as MS-DOS, and DEC VAX-11/VMS. It works best at editing small files (50Kb or less), and can edit many files simultaneously. Unlike other editors, which have separate command modes and input modes, MINED uses a modeless design for ease of use. It also includes powerful regular expressions for both searching and replacing text. MINED v3 (released 08/04/93) is available as CUG volume #399.

Overview of Volumes 200–299

Descriptions for volumes 100 through 299 can be found on the accompanying CD-ROM. Look in `D:\DOCS\CAP_V100.DOC` and `D:\DOCS\CAP_V200.DOC`.

CUG #200 Small C Interpreter

CUG #201 MS-DOS System Support

CUG #202 KAREL for MS-DOS

CUG #203 YAM for MS-DOS

CUG #204 68000 C Compiler

CUG #205 Utilities VII

CUG #206 Checkbook Register Doc. and Exec.

CUG #207 Checkbook Register Doc. and Source

CUG #208 'e' for CP/M 68K

CUG #209 Simplex Curve Fitting

CUG #210 Simulation and Loadable BIOS for CP/M

CUG #211 Search, Sort and Merge

CUG #212 Simulation for BDS

CUG #213 Van Nuys Enhancements

CUG #214 File Display Utilities

CUG #215 BBS for BDS C

CUG #216 Zmodem & Saveram

CUG #217 Spell and Dictionary, Part I

CUG #218 Spell and Dictionary, Part II

CUG #219 6502 Cross-Assembler

CUG #220 Windows Boss

CUG #221 6809 C for Flex

CUG #222 Small C v2.7 Exec. and Doc.

CUG #223	Small C v2.7 Source
CUG #224	UTILIX
CUG #225	Utilities and Zmath
CUG #226	ART-CEE
CUG #227	Portable Graphics
CUG #228	Miscellany IX
CUG #229	Little Smalltalk, Part I, with bundled files
CUG #230	Little Smalltalk, Part II, with bundled files
CUG #231	Little Smalltalk, Part I, with unbundled files
CUG #232	Little Smalltalk, Part II, with unbundled files
CUG #233	Make and Other Utilities
CUG #234	XDIR
CUG #235	Overview
CUG #236	Highly Portable Utilities
CUG #237	GRAD Graphics Doc and Lib
CUG #238	GRAD Graphics Source and Font
CUG #239	PC Gammon for MSC4
CUG #240	PC Gammon for Turbo C
CUG #241	Inference Engine and Rule Based Compiler
CUG #242	Still More Cross-Assemblers
CUG #243	DECUS C Preprocessor
CUG #244	deBruijn
CUG #245	Linear Cellular Automata
CUG #246	Cycles, Mandelbrot Graphics
CUG #247	MIRACL
CUG #248	MicroSPELL
CUG #249	C Spot Run (CSR) Library
CUG #250	68K FP Library & Mandelbrot Graphics
CUG #251	Pull Down Menus and Adventure System
CUG #252	C Tutor Doc.
CUG #253	C Tutor Source
CUG #254	Withdrawn from the CUG #Library
CUG #255	EGA Graphics Library

CUG #256	DeSmet Carry Routines
CUG #257	C Tutor Doc. and Exec. (Turbo C)
CUG #258	C Tutor Source (Turbo C)
CUG #259	Console I/O & Withers Tools
CUG #260	Zmodem, cu and tty Library
CUG #261	68 Cross-Assembler, MS-DOS
CUG #262	Ramey Tools
CUG #263	C_wndw Toolkit
CUG #264	NRO & Other PC Tools
CUG #265	cpio
CUG #266	microPLOX
CUG #267	8085, 2650 & S6 Cross-Assemblers
CUG #268	Unicorn Library (Turbo C)
CUG #269	Unicorn Library (MSC 4)
CUG #270	Miscellany X
CUG #271	Steven's Library (Turbo C)
CUG #272	Steven's Library (Datalight)
CUG #273	Turbo C Utilities
CUG #274	Arrays for C
CUG #275	Linear Cellular Automata II
CUG #276	Z80 and 6804 Cross-Assemblers
CUG #277	HP Plotter Library
CUG #278	CXL v5.1
CUG #279	CROBOTS
CUG #280	Software Tools Source
CUG #281	Unicorn Library v5.1
CUG #282	Quip and Graphics
CUG #283	FAFNIR
CUG #284	Portable 8080 System
CUG #285	Bison for MS-DOS
CUG #286	GRAD for MSC
CUG #287	GRAD for Turbo C
CUG #288	Traveling Salesman, SD and Master Environment Access

CUG #289   Othello

CUG #290   Flex for MS-DOS

CUG #291   JJB for QC and TC

CUG #292   ASxxxx Cross-Assemblers

CUG #293   3-D Medical Imaging, Source

CUG #294   3-D Medical Imaging, Sample Imaging

CUG #295   **blkio Library**

CUG #296   C to C++ Migrator

CUG #297   Small Prolog

CUG #298   PC Curses

CUG #299   MEL and BP

Overview of Volumes 100–199

CUG #126	Martz Library
CUG #127	RAP (A Text Formatter) v2.21
CUG #128	ROFF4 v1.61
CUG #129	CITADEL v2.10a
CUG #130	BIOS Utilities
CUG #131	ACRL
CUG #132	6809 Tools, 6809 C Compiler and Graphics Driver
CUG #133	'e' Screen Editor v4.0
CUG #134	Compiler Utilities
CUG #135	VLI: Very Long Integer
CUG #136	Games III
CUG #137	DDJ #1
CUG #138	DDJ #2
CUG #139	KAREL the Robot v1.00
CUG #140	Miscellany II
CUG #141	Miscellany III
CUG #142	Boulton Catalog Volume
CUG #143	Van Nuys Tools
CUG #144	Van Nuys Tools Doc.
CUG #145	ROFF4 v1.6P
CUG #146	Small C for 6800, for Flex Operating System
CUG #147	RBBS v4
CUG #148	TMS9900/99000 Cross-Assemblers
CUG #149	6800/1802 Cross-Assemblers (Portable Version)
CUG #150	Extractions from PC-SIG #50 and #142
CUG #151	Ed Ream's Screen Editor for MS-DOS
CUG #152	C Utilities for MS-DOS
CUG #153	C Utilities for MS-DOS
CUG #154	PC Tools
CUG #155	B-Trees, FFT, ONED & Util I
CUG #156	Small C with Floats
CUG #157	QE for MS-DOS, CMODEM, FWT, TP
CUG #158	QE for BDSC

CUG #159   Adventure for MS-DOS

CUG #160   Programs from "Learning to Program in C"

CUG #161   Programs from "Efficient C"

CUG #162   Mchip80

CUG #163   Small C for MS-DOS

CUG #164   Windows for C

CUG #165   Programs from "Reliable Data Structures"

CUG #166   CUG Directory

CUG #167   Windows, UNIX-Like Utility

CUG #168   Simple Database

CUG #169   Miscellany IV

CUG #170   Miscellany V

CUG #171   Miscellany VI

CUG #172   Lex, Part I

CUG #173   Lex, Part II

CUG #174   Withdrawn from the CUG #Library

CUG #175   Withdrawn from the CUG #Library

CUG #176   XLISP v1.6

CUG #177   Dr. Shaw's DOS Shell

CUG #178   TVX Source

CUG #179   TVX Doc. and Executable

CUG #180   Withdrawn from the CUG #Library

CUG #181   CFORUM and LZW

CUG #182   UNIX BBS

CUG #183   PC Tool II

CUG #184   RUNAND

CUG #185   SORTS

CUG #186   MAKE and AIM

CUG #187   Functions IV

CUG #188   Utilities VI

CUG #189   PC Tools III

CUG #190   Steve Passe's 68Kb Assembler

CUG #191   Miscellany VII

CUG #192   Miscellany VIII
CUG #193   Crypto Toolbox
CUG #194   JUGPDS 17
CUG #195   JUGPDS 18
CUG #196   JUGPDS 19
CUG #197   MicroEMACS v3.9, Exec. and Doc.
CUG #198   MicroEMACS v3.9, Source
CUG #199   GED

Subject Keyword Index

Contents

Title Index

Platform (OS/CPU) Index

Foreword

The platform associated with each CUG volume indicates the general computing environments (CPU and/or operating systems) it supports. Here are some examples:

- A program running on three or more UNIX platform systems will also earn the generic platform designation of UNIX (e.g., DEC Ultrix, HP-UX, and Solaris).
- A program running on four or more platforms will earn the distinction of "Highly Portable."
- A Cross-Assembler that runs under MS-DOS and creates 6800 Assembly language as output will be listed under both MS-DOS and 6800.
- If a program runs under Windows 3.1, Windows95, and has no platform-specific features (e.g., 32-bit API calls), it will be designated under the lowest-common denominator (Windows 3.1).
- No distinction is made between *any* Intel or compatible brands of CPUs unless a Pentium (or better) is required.

Contents

Appendix A: How to Contribute to the CUG Library

The C/C++ Users' Group is continually looking for the best freeware and shareware tools to improve the CUG Library. Any tool or library that is written primarily in ANSI C or C++ is eligible for inclusion. Programs need not be massive nor unique for inclusion. Improvements to existing programs that improve portability are also encouraged. Source archives can be individual or collaborative efforts.

Authors who wish to submit their own work should ideally fax or send by postal mail a completed Author's Release form (see following page) first. E-mail inquiries are welcome, but an Author's Release form must be received before an evaluation can take place. You should receive a definite answer within 30 days of sending in your submission.

In most cases, you need not send in media of any kind (disks or tapes). If the source code is available via FTP or HTTP (web) servers, CUG will download the latest version directly from the site indicated on the Author's Release form. If a dedicated Internet server is not available and the archived package is smaller than 1MB, then you can submit the software via uuencoded e-mail attachments. If none of these options is practical, then you may submit the software on 1.44MB MS-DOS readable diskettes. For ease of transfer, CUG requires that archive (e.g., ZIP) files be no larger than 1.44MB each. A submission can consist of any number of archive files, as long as each fits within this limit.

CUG is currently on a schedule of updating the CUG Library CD-ROM twice yearly. New editions are released in January and July with, closing dates for new submissions roughly in March and September respectively. Due to administrative overhead, only a limited number of changes can go into each new edition of CUG Library CD-ROM. Thus, you may have to wait for the following update to see your archive in print.

As a small token of our appreciation, you'll receive a complimentary of the next edition of CUG CD-ROM if your submission is accepted.

AUTHOR's RELEASE FOR CUG LIBRARY CD-ROM CONTRIBUTION

The C/C++ Users' Group welcomes submissions for inclusion in the CUG Library CD-ROM. We cannot distribute your submission without this release. All fields (except FTP and WWW) must be filled. Phone and fax numbers are for CUG internal use only and are not published.

NAME _____

ADDRESS _____

_____

CITY _____ STATE _____ ZIPCODE _____

COUNTRY _____

PHONE_____ FAX _____

E-MAIL_____ FTP_____

WWW _____

DESCRIPTION OF SUBMITTED MATERIALS:

The submitted materials are (check only one):

_____   (Someone Else's Public Domain or Shareware)
         To the best of my knowledge currently in the public domain or authorized for distribution as shareware.

_____   (My Public Domain)
         Written by me and hereby placed into the public domain. Permission is hereby granted to the C/C++ Users' Group to distribute the submitted materials freely for noncommercial personal use.

_____   (My Shareware)
         Written by me and protected by certain copyright restrictions clearly specified in the files constituting the submission. Permission is hereby granted to The C/C++ Users' Group to distribute the submitted materials, without royalty or other compensation, and to charge their normal distribution fee for such distribution, provided that my copyright restrictions are included unchanged in each copy distributed.

Signed: _____ Date: _____

The C/C++ Users' Group (CUG) collects, maintains, and distributes C/C++ source code, publishes in *The C/C++ Users Journal,* and serves as a resource for C/C++ users.

URL http://www.HAL9K.com/cug
e-mail sysop@HAL9K.com

Please fill out, sign, and return this form by fax to (313) 663-6861 or snail mail to:

Victor R. Volkman, CUG ACQ ED
P.O. Box 130206
Ann Arbor, MI 48113-0206
USA

Appendix B: CD-ROM Layout

Here is a list of important files and directories:

readme.txt	This file.
setup.exe	Windows 3.1/NT/95 Setup program.
htmldocs/	Root directory for offline web browsing.
htmldocs/index.htm	CUG offline Home Page for web browsing.
htmldocs/title.htm	Index of CUG volumes by Title.
htmldocs/subject.htm	Index of CUG volumes by Subject.
htmldocs/platform.htm	Index of CUG volumes by Operating System or CPU.
htmldocs/author.htm	Index of CUG volumes by Author Name.
htmldocs/language.htm	Index of CUG volumes by Language (C/C++/ASM/etc.).
htmldocs/whatsnew.htm	What's New at the CUG.
viewhtml/i-view.exe	I-VIEW Offline web browser.
vol_100/	CUG Library volumes 100-199.
vol_200/	CUG Library volumes 200-299.
vol_300/	CUG Library volumes 300-399.
vol_400/	CUG Library volumes 400-478.
winzip/setup.exe	Install program for WinZip and WinZip 95.

WinZip

An Easier ZIP for Windows 3.1 and Windows 95

The ZIP file format, first introduced in PKZIP by PKWARE, Inc. (Brown Deer, WI), has become the industry's de facto standard for both grouping and compressing files. ZIP files use a variety of compression methods to reduce plain text files up to 80% and executable files about 50%. A single ZIP file can contain hundreds of compressed files with complete subdirectory information. When required, a ZIP file can span multiple floppies and provide simple password-protected encryption. WinZip, by Nico Mak Computing, Inc., makes handling complex archive files as simple as a point-and-click. As I hope you will see, using ZIP files with WinZip is even easier than using unzipped files.

To install WinZip now, choose File|Run from Program Manager and enter:

```
d:\winzip\setup
```

where d: is your CD-ROM drive. Answer the installation dialogs with default parameters. This is a version of WinZip that automatically detects whether you are running Windows 3.1 or Win32 platform and selects the correct install from the two subdirectories in the \winzip subdirectory on the CD-ROM.

- There are several ways to open an archive with WinZip:
- Double-click on an archive listed in the Windows File Manager
- Drag-and-drop an archive onto WinZip
- Use File|Open and follow the standard open dialog
- Right-click on the desktop (Windows 95 only)
- Right-click on a filename (Windows 95 Explorer only)

The main WinZip window features a list box with the names, sizes, and date/time stamps of all files in the open archive (Figure A.1). This list can be scrolled and sorted on any field. A toolbar provides fast access to commonly used actions. All options (including window size and position) can be saved and restored. Extensive context-sensitive help is always available.

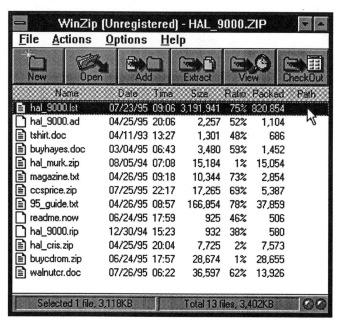

Double-clicking on a file in the WinZip main window follows the same convention as double-clicking in the File Manager. First the file is extracted from the archive. If the file is executable, it is run; otherwise, the file is opened by the appropriate application based on standard Windows associations (for example, Windows Write for *.wri files).

WinZip fully supports the Windows drag-and-drop interface as both client and server: you can drag-and-drop files from WinZip to other applications. WinZip extracts the files before dropping them on the target application. The target application treats the files as if they had been dropped by the File Manager. You can also drop archives on WinZip to open them or drop files on WinZip to add them to the open archive.

Install and Uninstall Directly from ZIP File

WinZip streamlines the process of installing and uninstalling software distributed in archives to its simplest possible form. This feature can also save megabytes of disk space by tracking and removing all traces of an application. WinZip runs the installation program of an archived application, gives you a chance to try the program, and optionally offers to restore your system to its original state. The uninstall step can selectively remove directories, files, icons, or program groups created by an install program and can restore any altered .ini files. You have complete control over the uninstall process, and no changes are made without approval.

If an archive does not have an install or setup program, you can use the CheckOut facility to easily try the files in the archive. The CheckOut facility extracts all files and creates a program group with icons for all or some files. Just double-click on an icon in the CheckOut group to view the corresponding file with the appropriate application. WinZip optionally deletes the CheckOut files and program group.

WinZip requires Windows 3.1 or later. No other programs are required for basic operations involving ZIP files. Optional features require one or more external programs, including the PKZIP and PKUNZIP product from PKWARE, Inc., lha.exe from Haruyasu Yoshizaki, or the Shareware ARJ product from Robert Jung. WinZip interfaces to several programs to access ARC files and optionally runs most virus-scanning utilities. See the online help for details.

Documentation, Licensing, and Support

WinZip provides extensive documentation in a Windows Help file. Nico Mak includes an exhaustive list of procedures providing every possible operation you might want to do to a ZIP file. Full coverage of how WinZip interfaces to third-party products such as PKZIP, Norton Desktop for Windows, and McCaffee virus scanners is also thoroughly covered.

Because WinZip is marketed as shareware, you may evaluate it for up to 21 days for free. If you decide that WinZip is useful and plan to use it beyond the evaluation period, you must register. You can register directly with the author, via CompuServe SWREG forum, or through the Public Software Library (PsL). Readers of this book can use the special coupon for $5 off registration (provided in the back of the book). Registered users receive a disk with the latest version of the product.

Nico Mak provides technical support to registered users via e-mail. Registered users are entitled to download beta test versions by FTP.

Support Resources

e-mail:	support@winzip.com
	70056.241@compuserve.com
CompuServe:	GO WINZIP
FTP:	ftp://ftp.winzip.com/winzip/
WWW:	http://www.winzip.com/winzip/

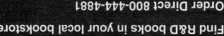

Standard C Date/Time Library
Programming the World's Calendars and Clocks
by Lance Latham

Standard C
Date/Time Library
Programming the World's
Calendars and Clocks

A Complete Date/Time Toolkit

Does the year 2000 have you sweating late-night code? Use our complete library of C programming functions to master 'Y2K', time on the net, ISO 8601, time stamp compression, or any other time/date application you encounter. Using the Julian Day as a common denominator between the world calendars, Lance Latham has solved the conversion of virtually all (including the Chinese!) the world calendars. Need to convert dates in the Maya calendar to the Khárizmian calendar? Plug in the modules, write a few lines of code, and away you go! All of this, together with basic western calendar/clock applications, are provided in straightforward, legible C. CD-ROM included. 576 pp, ISBN 0-87930-496-0.

RD2735 $49.95

Programming the Parallel Port
Interfacing the PC for Data Acquisition and Process Control
by Dhananjay V. Gadre

Programming
the Parallel Port
Interfacing the PC for Data Acquisition
and Process Control

Using the PC for Data acquisition or control? *Programming the Parallel Port* gives you a smart (and inexpensive) way to interface your data acquisition hardware to the PC – and includes complete code for a Linux-based system. You'll start with a thorough discussion of the interface connection, then move on to more advanced topics – including examinations of interface design. Key topics include: the Enhanced Parallel Port (EPP), Extended Communications Port (ECP), Analog/Digital Converters (ADC and DAC), adding bits to the parallel port, hosting an EPROM emulator, connecting the parallel port to an external microprocessor, and generating digital waveforms. Disk included, 320 pp, ISBN 0-87930-513-4

RD2739 $44.95

μC/OS The Real-Time Kernel
by Jean J. Labrosse

μC/OS explains the design and implementation of the Micro-Controller Operating System – a real-time kernel with performance comparable to many commercially available kernels! This system can manage up to 64 tasks and is written in C with assembly language for maximum portability. Jean Labrosse takes you through the fundamentals of a multitasking real-time system, including discussions of: kernel concepts; kernel structure; interrupt processing; communication, synchronization, and coordination; and initialization and configuration. You also get appendices covering the complete code, a port for the Intel 80186/80188, and an overview of real-time kernel manufacturers. Disk included, 266 pp, ISBN 0-87930-448-8.

RD2352 $49.95

μC/OS
The Real-Time Kernel

Jean J. Labrosse

Third Printing Revised for v.1.08